Total
Sex

Total Sex

An Illustrated Guide to the Ultimate Pleasures of Physical Love

Dan Abelow

BERKLEY BOOKS, NEW YORK

TOTAL SEX

A Berkley Book / published by arrangement with
the author

PRINTING HISTORY
Eight previous Charter printings
Ninth printing / January 1983
Berkley edition / January 1988

ISBN: 0-425-11205-5

A BERKLEY BOOK ® TM 757,375
Berkley Books are published by The Berkley Publishing Group,
200 Madison Avenue, New York, New York 10016.
The name "BERKLEY" and the "B" logo
are trademarks belonging to Berkley Publishing Corporation.

PRINTED IN THE UNITED STATES OF AMERICA

30 29 28 27 26 25 24 23 22 21 20

TABLE OF CONTENTS

CONTENTS

CONTENTS

CONTENTS

V. Enjoying All Life's Loves at Once

Total Sex

Ready for Something New?

What could be new in sex? You can lie on your stomach, your back, your side. Even standing on your head isn't new. Sex has been around for a long time. But now it's your turn.

There is a lot in this book that will be new **to you.** If you're still looking for the fireworks in sex, you'll find them in Chapter Two. If you're past fireworks, it's doubtful that you know all about orgasmic explosions. It's always great to learn a new way to reach an ultimate orgasm. The middle of the book is devoted to them.

Do you know the art of being a continually better lover? This is how you become a much better lover two years from now than you are today. No matter how much you know, your sexuality can be expanded.

For example, society is loosening up. Do you know how to enjoy all life's loves at once? Aha! Now that's something you can always learn more about!

There are more horizons you can cross: Do you want to know how to release your deepest desires? How to bring back the thrill when it has gone? How to expand your tenderness, sensitivity, and eagerness? How to enjoy the lushness of pure sensuality? How to find total release in ecstasy? How to enjoy several new kinds of orgasms?

But there's still more. It's something special, and that's you. Once you realize how much your sexual growth can accelerate, loving can become more intense and exciting than it's ever been before. There are new sensations to enjoy. New ways to expand your pleasures. A new chance to become closer to your lover.

What's new in sex? As an individual you can lift your sexual happiness to a new height. Are you ready to try?

The Rise of the Ex-Puritan

The majority of Americans are ex-Puritans. What caused this transformation? The minority who are promiscuous did not change. They only came out from behind closed doors. The real change was the people who cast off their inhibitions. These people made a new discovery. Accepting the body's natural sensuality offers many meaningful pleasures. They realized that rejecting pleasure is a lower standard of personal honesty.

What gave them the freedom to break their inhibitions? Our civilization has produced planetwide pollution, one-button nuclear extinction, boring jobs, corrupt leaders, and discovery of billions of light years of intergalactic void. Mobility dissolves the sense of community. Advertising stimulates desires. Media introduce more exciting ways to live. Most people learn to say good-bye again and again without shedding more than a single, lonely tear.

These shifts may be mutually supporting: inner freedom expands as the outer society declines. A Kingdom within was found in the Spring woods: midst earth and trees, grass and sunlight, two heads turned as one and kissed—and discovered that life is reborn with excitement when it is sparked with the urgency of love.

13

Why do people become ex-Puritans? Because genuine moments of pure happiness await them . . . because the sound of a loving voice reawakens one's eagerness for life . . . because love and sensuality counterbalance the horrors of our age . . . because "everything" can depend on one's good fortune to find love. These are not answers to the world's problems, but a natural and strong sexuality can open a meaningful world when no other exists. It gives millions an attainable way to renew themselves and enjoy being alive.

The Need for an Exciting Freedom

Once sexual freedom was discovered it spread rapidly, perhaps because millions found it a rewarding challenge. Daily life is routine and often stifling. The dreams of youth and middle age are beaten down by limited opportunities. Women face even smaller opportunities. Most of the few who "get ahead" move upward only when they make unsettling compromises. Frustration is common. Practically no one feels at ease.

A challenge of worth and meaning is a welcome relief. Sexual freedom may be a critical outlet for many people. Handling it well produces a sense of responsibility and integrity. Not only does it offer personal growth but it provides physical and emotional rewards few other areas of society can match.

The Inside Secret

Today a man and woman can meet in the afternoon and be in bed together by evening. It depends on their mood and chemistry. This isn't sex for its own sake. If it's right, it's right—and both know it.

A decade ago, this kind of freedom was new. Anything and everything was welcome. It was time to explore satiation. A variety of books helped people improve their performance. Since then, norms have changed. The monogamous lifetime marriage has become the exception. Swinging has been institutionalized as a multi-million dollar business. Sexual experimentation has soared into one of the nation's leading recreational sports.

Millions probably can't remember how many men or women they screwed and all the kind of kinky sex they tried. Many of those who only experimented with one partner reached a limit to their ability to go farther. After their divorce, they often found it the same. When pleasure is mainly physical, there is a limit to the satisfaction the body provides.

There aren't any more new places to go physically—at least for those who have tried all the places. Then where is the next place to go? Into the head, the mind and heart of the man and woman behind the act. This inner direction is understandable. People feel so much frustration that they are reaching out wherever someone will touch them with sincerity and warmth, give them a chance to be happy, and return them to the purity of love.

Love's Sensitivity

New love relationships are very fragile. This is as true in a 25 year marriage which is trying to give new life to its love as for a man and woman who have just met. Each couple has to shape its relationship to its own needs and nurture it carefully. Emotional, physical, and mental communication are as important as love itself. If the relationship is to work, it also needs friendship and companionship.

Each partner should be open to spontaneous desires and variations the other might express. Help your partner let him or herself out, and don't hold yourself back. Don't ever assume your partner doesn't want intercourse when you do. Try it. If he or she feels it's right, you won't have to coax at all—you'll be there together.

Gradually, each partner's sensitive, private self emerges. Then you start making it with subtle expressions of tenderness and affection. The nuances become more important than almost anything else, because they give your love its meaning and value.

A Quiet Welcome for the Sexually Aggressive Woman

Men have been blessed with sexual freedom while women have been chained by a double standard. A man's sexual appetite was considered part of his masculinity. He was a "great lover" when he achieved a "conquest". Until recently a woman with a strong sexual drive was considered, to put it plainly, a slut.

The 180° turn we have recently made is long overdue. It has become respectable to be an admittedly sexually responsive woman, a human being with full sexual rights. Men have had to grow up too. Now both men and women stand revealed as vulnerable human beings first and as sexual equals—not objects —second.

This has released many women's sexual aggressiveness. Instead of running from their sexuality, they revel in it. New experiences, new partners, and letting go without restraint aren't things to avoid. With relaxed understanding new things usually turn out to be more familiar than they seem. Each new experience soon becomes passé, and the next experience becomes the challenge.

Enjoying the Male and Female Orgasm

Freedom is sometimes complicated. Now that sex is natural, honest, and open, some want to set up a new performance standard. On the contrary, freedom means individualized standards that satisfy personal needs. Being natural is sexy for some, while being kinky is the answer for others. There is also swinging, remaining single with multiple partners, homosexuality, serial monogamy, or a traditional lifetime marriage. Sexual freedom is not an ideal. It is a wide spectrum that offers many kinds of genuine satisfactions.

The new desire to enjoy orgasms has become a problem simply because more people want more of them. The equal right of women to sexual filfillment is sometimes taken too far, when the achievement of effortless multiple orgasms is used to measure a woman's sexuality. This problem is mirrored in men who regard the number of their orgasms as a measure of their performance.

The frequency and intensity of orgasms varies from person to person. Some people writhe and scratch uncontrollably. Others just tense their muscles then relax completely. This is not the only purpose of sex. Possessing a sensitive ability to turn on and satisfy your lover is more important than either the intensity or frequency of orgasms.

When performance is at stake, reduced enjoyment is often the consequence. If you constantly judge your lover's level of excitement, you may never relax enough to enjoy yourselves fully. If you attach your self-image to "curing" this problem, the frustration will stab your relationship in the heart. Concentrate instead on how at ease you are when you are closest to your partner. Take care of the quality of your loving and the orgasms should take care of themselves.

The Search for Additional Pleasures

It isn't surprising that unreasonably high expectations often accompany too small a contribution. If a couple is trying to expand their pleasures by trying new things frequently, they know their limitations and potentials. Many couples do not have this self-knowledge because they are unable to constantly introduce new sexual pleasures to each other. As a result, they become bored. Their expectations remain high, but their contribution will not produce the satisfactions they want.

Once sexual stagnation begins, the whole relationship can deteriorate. How common is this problem? Sexual boredom is often cited as a main cause of marital unhappiness.

Sex is more than a release from tension. The couple that satisfies each other in only three or four ways barely knows how to please each other. The fact that they can bring each other off in more than one way is an excellent indicator for the future. Actual progress is more important. If they don't get past the starting gate and move forward they may not stay satisfied much longer.

The Goal of Total Satisfaction

Sexual freedom is only one step in a longer journey, but it produced a valuable change: the limited man-woman roles of the past have diminished. Many couples are now exploring a more equal and open intimacy. Women are assuming an equal responsibility for the quality of lovemaking. Pleasure can expand because there are many more possibilities than when the man was dominant and the woman passive.

Today, men and women are looking for the same thing, even though they release themselves in different ways. Many men only need a naked woman in front of them. Going to bed with practically any woman is self-explanatory. Some men need deeper emotional contact.

21

That Special Tingling Anticipation

It's a hot summer afternoon. The sun hangs laxily in a cloudless sky, burning off time and identity. Two lovers lie by the river's edge, on an isolated patch of beach, or surrounded by thick woods. Eyes closed, they give themselves up to the solitude and companionship. A soft breeze tickles their skin with its cool fingers. He sits up and looks at her. She half-opens her eyes and smiles. There isn't any need to talk. Everything is understood. He leans over to kiss her and finds her tongue as willing and eager as his own.

Making love is more than an act. There is a tingling anticipation, the delicious sensation that someone is going to touch you deep inside, free your hidden yearnings, and make you fully alive.

Up Against a Naked Animal

Nature has used millions of years of evolution to perfect the sexual organs of men and women. They are incredibly well developed for providing pleasure and achieving a complete union. The whole body becomes involved during sex: the muscular system, nervous system, the glands, the heart and lungs work harder, the mind contributes its share. As passion builds, all the systems of the body become more and more aroused.

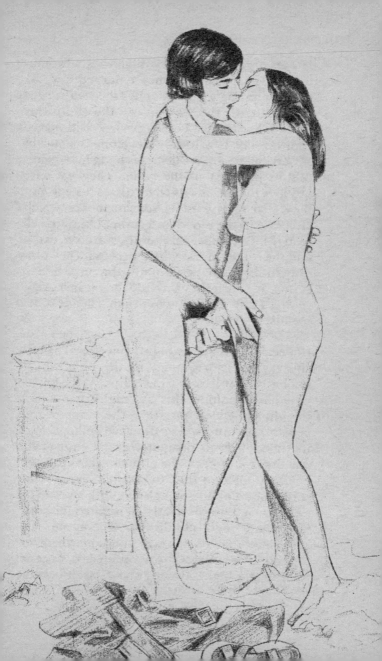

His sex organs respond visibly to sexual stimulation. His penis becomes enlarged and extends at an angle that matches the structure of the vagina in the woman. At the end of his penis is the glans. This is packed with nerve endings and is a highly developed center of sexual pleasure. Two testicles hang in the scrotum at the back of the penis. They not only produce the sperm which fertilizes her egg, but they also release male sex hormones which circulate in the blood and compel him to seek sexual intercourse. His genitals are the cause and the center of the whole process. They produce the hormonal stimulants that urge him to coitus, and then they provide the pleasure that rewards him for following their chemical demands.

Her sex organs are as highly developed as his. Her vagina is surrounded by the vulva which has both outer lips and inner lips. At the upper junction of the inner lips is a small organ called the clitoris which parallels the glans of the penis. It is saturated with nerve endings, and its function is to promote sexual enjoyment and orgasm. In fact, the clitoris seems to have no other function than to provide sexual pleasure. The vagina itself is lined with a group of muscles that are perfectly structured for both intercourse and childbirth. These muscles have specialized folds which enable them to expand to accommodate a large penis, or contract to grip tight a small one. Since they adjust automatically to the size of the penis, no men need fear their personal difference in size, since nature has provided for these differences. Not only is the vagina slanted to fit perfectly around the penis, but its muscles are specialized so that they provide the closest sort of physical union imaginable.

It might be thought that this supreme closeness would cause excessive friction, but nature has solved this problem in a way that adds to the pleasure and brings emotions into the relationship. The inner vulva contains glands which provide a lubricating fluid when a woman is sexually stimulated. This fluid first enables a penis to make an easy entrance, then it sensitizes the constant contact that is maintained between the penis and the walls of the vagina.

This natural lubrication of the vagina reveals evolution's most subtle magic. If sufficient foreplay does not precede the entrance of the penis, there will not be this state of moist readiness in the vagina and penetration will be difficult. The physical act provides a seemingly purposeful role for the emotions during this period of foreplay. In fact, this period of caressing, kissing, fondling, touching, and affection turns out to be one of the most important moments in almost every relationship. It contributes to the intensity of a couple's feelings for each other, and makes the coitus which

25

follows an experience of joy. Far from being a mistake, the foreplay which produces the lubrication introduces a profound and deep communication. Its ultimate value may be to preserve the union outside the bedroom, perhaps throughout the entire life of two people, making both the family and child rearing much more successful than they would be otherwise.

The Environment Includes You

The pleasantness of the surroundings is very important, though this is far from always true. It is difficult to relax in a messy bedroom or in a home that looks like it has been swirled in a tornado. The environment also includes the people who will be making love. A clean body is often as important as pleasant surroundings. Strong body odors or dirtiness can intrude on thoughts and feelings of affection. Finally, privacy is an important part of the romantic environment because it is essential for complete abandon. If one of the partners feels that they will "wake the children" or that someone who is not supposed to be there will walk in, this may dampen the sexual response. If there are problems in any of these areas, a couple should discuss and resolve them so that they can turn their attention to loving each other.

Most women want romantic and intellectual justification. They need a rationale for sex: who, why, sincerity, a couple's relationship to each other, willingness, and tenderness are all important. Other women simply decide whom they want.

But when a man and woman are in bed together—however their relationship started —they turn out to be more alike than different. They share common sexual goals, and these goals are expanding. People want more than they ever wanted before. They want to try to go all the way. How is this achicved?

The First Magic Touch

"What are the best places to be touched?" she asked. She was just divorced and a bit anxious. Her young husband had only known about his pleasure—not hers. Now she wanted to learn more about her body.

He explained that the erogenous zones are the most sensitive places to be touched. He started to list them but she interrupted. "Would you show me?" she asked.

She took off almost all her clothes and leaned back on the couch. He moved next to her and began kissing her, whispering, "The first place is just behind the ear, along the hair line." He ran the tip of his tongue there, and his light touch produced a tingle. He followed this with

a series of lingering kisses, explaining, "the ear
. . . the earlobe should be nibbled . . . up and
down the side of the neck . . . across the upper
part of the shoulder . . . all over the breasts
. . . the nipples should be given a lot of attention . . . the front sides of the hips . . . the
lower belly." Her head had rolled back and she
was breathing deeply. He had her lie face down
on the couch so he could show her the places on
her back. He continued, "the back of the neck
. . . up and down the spine . . . the area where
the lower back merges with the buttocks . . .
sometimes the buttocks . . . the backs and insides of the thighs . . . sometimes the back of
the knees . . . the soles of the feet."

He rolled her over, pulling off her underpants,
then bent forward and gently kissed her mons
veneris. He heard a sharp intake of breath as he
kissed her lower, along the inner lips of her
vulva. Her deep breathing grew heavier when
his tongue touched her clitoris. He covered the
whole area of her vagina with gentle tongue
strokes, concentrating on her clitoris, and
brought her to a climax. Then he kissed her on
the lips and asked if she wanted to learn his
most sensitive places. She pulled his mouth
against hers and kissed him hungrily.

She remembered his kisses and covered his
body equally well with her own. She was slow
and tender. It was half an hour before she pulled his underpants down. Following his expla-
nation she guided her tongue over the head of

his penis, especially the ring around the head, then further down the shaft, all over the scrotum, and finally to the bridge between the scrotum and the anus. He pulled her up against him and they kissed for a while. "There's only one place left," he whispered. "I'll bet you know what it is." She smiled and sat across his lap facing him. "You're right," he said as she reached down and put his penis inside her.

Sensuous Cuddling

When two lovers cuddle, the whole body becomes a sex organ. Cuddling produces relaxation, increased sensitivity, and silent communication. It is stimulating before sex. Afterward it is relaxing and leads to sleep.

There are three main positions for cuddling. The first is primarily for before intercourse. Both partners face each other. Their bodies touch gently: cheeks, chest, genitals, thighs, and feet. Moving slowly, their arms hold each other close. There is a natural urge to rub against each other, to press together. Kissing, light nibbling and "nuzzling" with the nose or cheek adds to the closeness.

In the second position he lies on his back and she snuggles against his side, her head on his chest. She can gently explore his body with her hand. In the opposite of this, she lies on her back with him against her side. Light touches are a welcome part of cuddling.

After sex the lovers can lie on their sides against each other. The man curls himself around behind her. He can bury his nose in her hair and enjoy a maximum of intimate contact with her buttocks. After a while, they can roll over and she can curl around his back. The touch of her breasts on his back should feel great to both of them. These two positions create a relaxing feeling of security. It is easy to fall asleep wrapped in bliss.

A Time to Reap, A Time to Sow, A Time to Let Your Excitement Grow

Just before foreplay begins is one of the most enticing moments in sexual intercourse. When each lover first thinks of what is to come they become physically aroused. His penis grows erect. Her juices begin to flow. These physical reactions can begin before either touches the other, when two people are in love and enjoy sex together. Each becomes aroused merely by knowing that in a few minutes they will be beginning an intimate union.

Once foreplay begins, the outward touch transforms each lover inside. As each stimulates the other they are also stimulating themselves.

When he fondles her breasts his penis may grow harder. When she touches his penis, she may quiver inside and start breathing harder. Giving and receiving occur simultaneously. The arousal builds, until both lovers have readied themselves for consummation.

New Positions for the Missionaries

New positions produce different kinds of stimulation. Some positions will delay ejaculation and others will accelerate it. They can be used in any sequence you like. Experiment freely to decide what you prefer.

Oral Foreplay: Oral sex can be enjoyed individually or mutually. The sensations are usually stronger when it is individual. He lies between her legs, or she can kneel or lie between his legs. There are many variations possible. Easy tongue-vagina contact is produced when she lies on her stomach with one or two pillows under her hips. He kneels over her upper back, facing her feet. Then he bends forward, burying his head like the proverbial ostrich. The emotional contact between two lovers is intensified when oral love is mutual, as in sixty-nine. It is probably more comfortable to lie on your sides. The main problem with mutual kisses is that it becomes almost impossible to concentrate on your partner when you're about to reach orgasm.

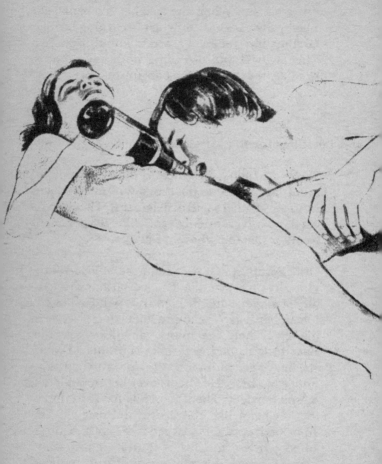

Sitting on Top: She can sit on top of him, either facing toward or away from him. This can be done in bed, in a rocking chair, or on a garden swing. When she faces him he can massage her breasts. After a while she can lean forward and stretch her legs out, whether she is facing him or facing away from him.

Doggy Style: This is a deep and stimulating way to make love. She leans forward on all fours and he enters her from behind. By putting the balls of his feet against the wall, he can strengthen his thrusts and deepen his penetration. She can also lean over a chair or table.

Rear Entry: Rear entry is very enjoyable when both partners lie on their sides, or if she lies on her stomach. Deeper penetration can usually be achieved in the latter position if she places one or two pillows under her hips. Once entry has been made, she can close her legs for tighter stimulation, and he can lie on top or kneel astride her while her legs are closed.

The Upside-down Missionary: This is the missionary position with her on top. This gives her control, and she can set the pace according to her growing excitement.

Sitting Up Together: They sit facing each other. She puts her legs around his waist and he slides into her as she moves closer. They wrap their arms around each other for support, or put their hands behind them on the bed. Intimate touching and kissing in this position are very pleasurable.

Clean All Over: Making love in the shower or bath makes some people feel clean and pure inside. Those who enjoy swimming will enjoy this.

The Fabulous Quickie

Once a man and a woman have become physically responsive to each other, the quickie enters their relationship. If they are lucky, quickies frequently bring lightning-like pleasure. It is a passionate embrace, usually completely clothed, that occurs suddenly. Looking down and watching can add a mood of raw sensuality.

The most common ways to enjoy quickies are standing against a wall or a tree; her leaning over a handy chair or table and being entered from the rear; or him sitting on a chair while she leans forward off his lap, being held by the hips. Two of the three favorite places for the quickie are around the house: the kitchen and the TV-room floor. The third is that ever popular mobile bedroom, the automobile. Whenever and wherever it strikes, the quickie adds something special to the day.

"That felt so good!"

A man may want to know when a woman he is loving has experienced an orgasm. A strong female orgasm can usually be felt by the penis because it includes muscular vaginal contractions. A milder orgasm produces a general relaxation of her whole body. If he is alert and learns from experience, he will come to know her unique orgasmic responses and he will be able to tell when she has experienced orgasm.

This isn't a difficult problem for her. His orgasm consists of a series of strong contractions of his penis accompanied by the ejaculation of sperm. His sexual excitement diminishes rapidly after his orgasm, and both his ejaculation and relaxation are unmistakable.

What Lies Beyond the Orgasm?

Just how good is it to slide one inch at a time, along that thirty-three feet? What thirty-three feet? If an average act of lovemaking takes 100 strokes and each stroke is four inches, then two lovers share 33 feet of intimate friction.

But how good is it? There is much more to intercourse than reaching orgasm. It is unfortunate that many people think of sex mainly as an opportunity to have an orgasm. Nearly anyone will serve that purpose. But once you are in love, once you have shared your first fifty orgasms, there is a lot you can do to expand your sexual relationship.

Physical sex can be a path to a wordless, deep, and sensitive contact. It creates the kind of relationship that sustains lovers through the hassels and trials of daily life. It is easier to show deep love and feel intense pleasure through lovemaking than in almost any other way. The intimacy and shared pleasure is often more rewarding than the orgasm itself.

The True Range of Your Sexual Potentials

Many sexually liberated men and women are using only a small fraction of their emotional and orgasmic potentials. The missing elements are their willingness to release their inner desires, and to accept that their sexuality is a vehicle to a new realm of genuine, intense pleasures.

This sexual growth comes in two stages. The first release comes from the discovery that there is someplace new to go. The physical horizon is once again reopened. This leads to new explorations and the enjoyment of fireworks. The second stage comes after the fireworks. Then they discover that there is an emotional horizon. This is a bigger challenge, but it can lead to the creation of explosions.

The Exploration of Joint Sensuality

Enjoying sex is one of the major recreational pursuits in our society. Yet many lovers know less about their partner's deepest sexual desires than their politics or TV habits. Keeping desires hidden is easy. No one wants to shock their partner. Unfortunately, this closes the physical horizon and limits emotional openness during intercourse. When one of them finally gathers his or her courage and admits, "I've always wondered what it would be like to try that," they frequently discover that their partner also wants to try new things.

When desires, fantasies, and dreams are hidden they do not disappear. Unseen hopes and fears play a role in shaping a relationship, even though they are secrets. A couple can make their relationship all they want it to be only when they bring their desires out into the open.

Couples should tell each other that a kiss on the lips is not all the kissing they want. Suppressed desires force people to make love in emotional darkness and then wonder why they fail to find the fireworks of sex. At the very least, they should admit that they want to taste the fireworks. Then they'll be ready to take the next step, trying to create them.

The Warm-Up: Turning Her On Physically

Greater contact between lovers is one of the keys to an intense sexual experience. Beginning with one way that he can free his woman from her inhibitions, we'll go to two ways she can turn him on, then jump right into a way they might touch each other deeply.

He should start with a basic concern for the mood and privacy. Two to three drinks, well spaced, will loosen you both up. Sit close and do a lot of touching—her hands, shoulders, neck, ears—occasionally brush across her nipples. When you stand next to her touch her fanny a little. After some touching pull her close. Kiss her the way you really mean it— long, lingering, playful. Give her loving kisses with a lot of tongue and the feeling that you like to kiss her. Let your hips tell her that you want her. Don't hold back or act embarrassed.

Kiss her like this several times over an hour or so. Do it once more then sit or lie her down. Continue kissing her while you open her blouse and play with her nipples. Let her know by the way you kiss her that you are carried away by the feel of her breasts.

"Fireworks" are only found once you begin doing all you would like. They are intensely personal and each couple has to develop their own arsenal. The fireworks offered here are a sample of the possibilities you can use to intensify your excitement—once you become willing to admit and share your needs.

As she becomes aroused unzip your fly and take out your penis. Take her hand in yours and put it around your penis, squeezing her hand gently. If she looks at you while you do this, look her right in the eye. The preliminaries are over. Your rocket should soon start to reach escape velocity.

The Secret Turn-on

This is an underhanded way for a woman to tell a man she wants him. It will blow all his gaskets at once. In a private moment (to obtain it, excuse yourself for a moment) insert your finger in your vagina. Hug him when you return, making sure to press his penis against your hips or side. As you do this put your arm around his neck and innocently pass your scented finger along his top lip, just under his nose. Chances are, either his eyes will pop out of his head or he'll choke on his heart which will have jumped into his throat. Whisper in a sultry voice that you can't wait until you get home. In less than 30 seconds the bulge in his pants will show you that he can't wait either.

The Ice Cube Trick

You can do this to your man anywhere drinks are available, but it works best in a bar or at home. After you finish your drink make sure he is watching you. Slip an ice cube between your lips. Let it pause there, then slowly suck it into your mouth. Look at him sensually while you do this. Move the ice cube around your slightly opened mouth with your tongue. He won't be able to take his eyes off you. Then slip the cube back to your lips so that it just pokes out. Drop it back into the glass, letting your tongue touch the edge of your lip for a second.

You've said it all with your mouth, tongue, and eyes. It's a message he won't be able to ignore.

The Most Passionate Hunger of All

Lovers who want to scale the heights of excitement inevitably discover oral sex. Good oral sex not only excites your partner—it turns you on when you give it. Any problems of distaste are in the mind. A few tries should dispel them.

Many men do not know how to perform cunnilingus properly. Long tongue strokes from the vagina to the clitoris are a good beginning. The clitoris is the most sensitive point and it should receive most of the attention. It should not be chewed, bitten, or sucked hard. If he has any trouble finding it he should ask for her guidance in finding it and in the best way to kiss, lick, and suck it. Neither will remember any embarrassment once she abandons herself in an orgasm.

41

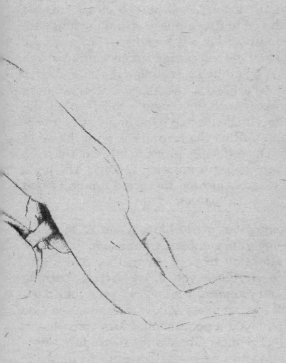

The better he becomes at cunnilingus the more orgasms she will probably have before intercourse begins. Then he need not fear leaving her unsatisfied during coitus, so he can time his orgasm to suit his needs.

When she kisses him she can either use her mouth and tongue alone or stimulate him with her mouth and hands together. The hands are important because many men cannot reach orgasm when being stimulated by the mouth alone. Gently suck the glans with the mouth or stroke it with the tongue while firmly holding the penis with one hand and gently grasping and pulling the scrotal sac with the other hand. Occasionally press firmly on the area between the scrotum and the anus. The prostrate gland is located there and it is saturated with sensitive nerves.

A spontaneous genital kiss is one of the most arousing gifts a man or woman can give. Care and attention to your partner help you give your best. When you enjoy giving, learning new and more exciting ways to get your partner off becomes easy. All women and men who have enjoyed a good genital kiss come to expect it. The most direct way to introduce this is to go down on your partner until he or she is nearly berserk. Then swing your legs around, gently push his or her head in the right direction, and say, "It's your turn now."

Sixty-nine, or mutual genital kissing, can last for minutes or hours. It is easier to last longer after he has had his first orgasm. This is an excellent way to return him to passionate intensity.

Since there may be questions on which oral technique gives your partner the greatest pleasure, you should occasionally guide your partner when kissing. No matter how much experience they have had, you are different. Once your lover has learned the best ways to satisfy you, you will realize that being able to teach them this is almost as important as being able to reach orgasm in the first place.

Grand Sexual Station

The clitoris is absolutely vital to her sexual fulfillment. Unless it is stimulated during intercourse, she might not have an orgasm. This doesn't mean that it has to be stimulated directly, by the penis or the finger. The nerves from the clitoris extend over the entire vulva and into the walls of the vagina. The penis stimulates the clitoris without touching it, while it is in the vagina.

This pea-shaped organ is located at the upper point of the vaginal opening, where the inner lips come together. When the penis is in the vagina its friction pulls the inner lips in and out of the vagina with each stroke. This pulls the lips back and forth over the clitoris, stimulating it.

A few women find it extremely exciting for the penis to be placed near the front of the vagina, so that the clitoris is directly massaged by each thrust. He can do this in many positions by adding a slight pressure in that direction. To

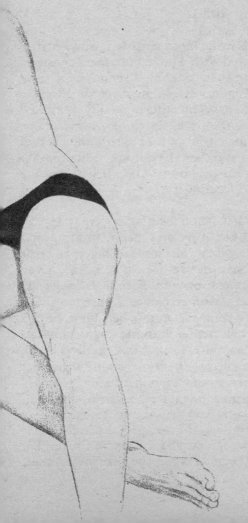

do this in the missionary position, for example, he should move his hips a little higher and forward, so that the top of his penis slides against her clitoris when he thrusts down.

How Does He Play with It?

The clitoris is the most sensitive point because it is saturated with a large number of sensitive nerve endings. In touching it, gentleness is important. Tenderness is much more effective than roughness. The clitoris should be stroked lightly with the tip of the finger, either in circular motions around it or across the hood of the clitoris and then the clitoris itself. Another way to stroke it is by twirling it between the thumb and forefinger.

As her clitoris is touched her legs may spread wider and her hips may begin rotating and thrusting against his hand. This is a clear signal of her desire for intercourse. Even though penetration at this time is easily accomplished, a woman can be aroused to greater intensity before he enters her. First, he can penetrate her vagina with his finger, simulating his penis with in and out motions. With patience he can find her best "spots" inside her vagina. These are located in different places in different women's vaginas, according to their individual physical sensations. There are usually at least one or two special places in the vagina that are very sensitive and bring her rapidly to orgasm when they are stimulated.

Those Unstoppable Hands!

If you stimulate several parts of your lover's body at once, it may well increase their pleasure. It certainly won't decrease it! Nor should the hands caress only the sexual organs, such as his penis or her vagina and breasts. Hands should wander freely and sensuously over the legs, buttocks, back, shoulders, and neck. Your fingers can run through your lover's hair, stroke their cheek, or tease the hair around the side of their genitals. The hands should tantalize and arouse while touching. Every part of the body that is within reach can be caressed, and this freedom to touch and be touched will heighten the feelings of giving and receiving.

Vary the Pace

Sam imagined that he was the best lover in the world. Janie and Ann always got off unbelievably with him. What was wrong with Sheila? She said there wasn't anything wrong with her. Sam didn't believe her. If she couldn't get off with him, it was her fault.

Sam couldn't possibly be the best because he's too shallow. The best sex is a total mind-body communication between emotionally open people. Reading your lover's responses is more important than any technique. This means knowing what to do and what not to do, including signalling your needs to your lover.

Sam not only didn't understand Sheila, he wouldn't believe she knew something he didn't. Sheila finally got through to him. She needed him to change his pace—to go slower in the beginning—and to do a couple of new things. In fact, she taught him a lot more than understanding.

One nice present you can give your lover is a change of pace—including in it something new you learn from a friend, read in a book, or fantasize. You shouldn't do this constantly (unless your lover likes lots of surprises), but if you don't do it occasionally, sex will become routine.

The range of new possibilities is larger than most people think. Humanity's "cultural inventory" of sexual practices is huge. You now enjoy only the known part of you. There is more of you to expose and develop. The more you learn and put into sex, the more you get out of it.

Would You Swear on a Blazing Vibrator?

Are vibrators very good? If used properly and not all the time, the answer is yes. Contrary to what many believe, the best place for a vibrator is the clitoris, not the vagina. What's more, the battery powered penis-shaped vibrator is not as good as the plug-in kind.

Will a blazing vibrator replace a man? Not at all. The sensations from a self-held vibrator are mechanical and impersonal. The sensations from a vibrator in the hand of your lover can be inexpressibly intimate. Picture being a man inside your mate, on the edge of ecstasy, then putting a vibrator on her clitoris. (If this is too intense, put a warm, damp towel over the tip of the vibrator.) She should come very quickly —the double stimulation sets her right off.

She can do him with a vibrator too. Lubricating jelly or a warm, damp towel reduces the intensity and heightens the pleasure. A mild description of how a man looks when a vibrator is being used properly is head rolled back, mouth open, moaning, with his arm thrown across his face.

Just as important to many couples, a vibrator gives a great body massage. Giving a really good massage with your hands can be tiring. If you want to trade massages but save your energy for lovemaking (which is a relaxing evening after you both have a long day at work), the vibrator is indispensable for giving a thorough massage.

If the massage is given before lovemaking, use the vibrator on the nipples, around the neck, chest, belly, insides of the arms and thighs, armpits, hollow of the back, soles and palms, scrotum, and the space between it and the anus. When you first try a vibrator you will feel its full intensity immediately, but this is just

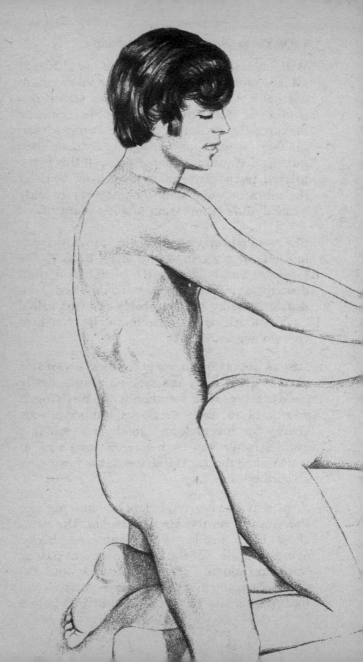

the beginning. Using it is a skill that comes with practice—and brings lots of pleasure as you learn.

The Deepest Penetration

The deepest penetration is simultaneously emotional and physical. The attitude of many people exemplifies this: "I've never had sex with someone I didn't feel deeply about." This doesn't mean that sexual experimentation isn't popular. Experimentation can achieve its greatest ease and variety in an open and accepting relationship. Both letting go and trying something intimate generally require trust. Even "sex for its own sake" is usually more enjoyable when it is with the person you care about the most.

The best of all sexual experiences occurs when two lovers get through to each other's hearts while making love. This ends all the anxieties about who is doing what to whom and why. Tenderness and sensitivity expand enormously when love is a deeply shared experience.

The Header

When the partner who is giving a genital kiss is in control this is fellatio or cunnilingus. When the genital partner is in control and is building to orgasm the technical name is irrumation, but we call it the header.

The best positions for the man are standing with her kneeling at his feet; with her lying on her back, a pillow under her head, and him kneeling over her chest; and lying on their sides facing each other. In the latter position he should be near one end of the bed because her feet will stick out the other end. He can bring his top leg over her shoulder and she can wrap her top arm around his back or press between the scrotal sac and the anus.

"Come and get me. I'm ready!"

How can a couple determine at what point in their foreplay he should enter her and begin coitus? Men who are sensitive to their lover often want to begin intercourse only when she is ready. This is another reason for being able to communicate openly during intercourse. There are many ways she can indicate her readiness, and her signalling him relieves him of any uncertainty that he might feel.

As the relationship develops they should learn to express clearly what they want when they

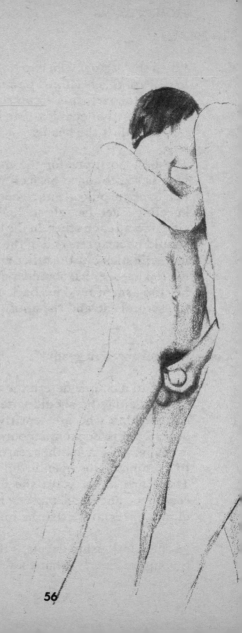

make love. Their goals will affect the time that he enters her. Sometimes they may want to reach the peak of their excitement together, in simultaneous orgasm. Other times he may want to make sure she is satisfied before he reaches orgasm. At still other times she may want to continue lovemaking after he has reached orgasm, with him giving her oral love until she is satisfied. She should also be solicitous of his desire to continue foreplay longer, if

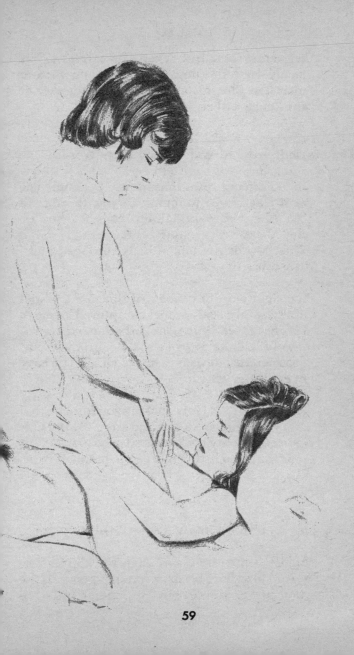

he wants that. But when she is ready, she should let him know that she wants him to enter her. Chances are, he won't want to wait any longer either.

The Magic Release of Well-Timed Dirty Words

"I could feel it building in her. Suddenly she went slack for a moment, then with a cry of 'Ahhhhh, I'm coming! I'm coming!' she exploded upward, arching her back. At the sound of her words my whole body throbbed and I joined her in ecstasy."

The right words at the right time are a sexual stimulant that can propel enraptured lovers to a higher level. When one or both partners use any of a wide variety of so-called dirty words at a passionate moment in intercourse it can have an explosive effect.

"Oh, Ginny . . . I love fucking you from behind . . . your cunt is so hot and wet . . . the way you squeeze my cock feels so gooooood . . . lift your ass just a little higher . . . unhhh, I like it, I like it . . ."

Something You've Probably Never Tried

Anal sex may be closer than you think. New sexual practices become commonplace all the time, just as oral sex grew in popularity during the last decade. In sex, you never know what is good until you try it.

For the man, her anus is a brand new, different place. It is tighter and firmer than the vagina. It grips a larger part of the shaft at once, and it can be contracted with more force than the vagina.

For the woman, this offers the pleasure of having another body cavity filled. The anus is an erogenous zone which contains many sensitive nerves. These may not be enough, alone, to bring a woman to orgasm, so either he or she can stimulate her clitoris at the same time.

There are three precautions to remember. First, both his penis and her anus should be well lubricated. Jelly is best, but Vaseline will work. Second, after his penis or finger has been in her anus it should not touch her vulva without being washed. Natural and harmless bacteria in the rectum can cause infections in the vagina. Third, he should make sure she is relaxed and in the mood by caressing her entire body.

He should take it easy because anal intercourse is sometimes painful. If she feels a bit of pain, he should stop moving while she relaxes her body. Then she should try pushing back against him when she is ready. A woman's mood directly affects her sensations. If she is uptight it will not be as good as when she is totally ready for it. Then it can be exquisitely pleasurable for both lovers.

The Water Bed Report

The water bed gets both a "superior" and a "frustrating" rating. There is an art to moving together on a water bed and some people prefer a firm mattress. The biggest problem is that the water bed moves the same way that you move. When you thrust forward there isn't any resistance to slide against. You go down and the bed goes down. Unless you are into the "rhythm" of the waves they roll back and knock you into the air when you don't expect it. The ripples extend beyond the bed: if you enjoy it less your lover gets upset, then he or she enjoys it less, which upsets you more.

A Stimulating Walk in the Garden

The best way to make a quiet bedroom boring is to make love in the woods on a bed of leaves, looking up at the sky, surrounded by singing birds and wind rustled branches. If you would like to have a memorable day outdoors, take your love for a spontaneous drive out to the woods. Bring along a shoulder bag that contains a soft blanket and an opened bottle of wine. Leave the car behind and take a few minutes to slowly walk a few hundred feet from the road, opening your senses to the thick smells, towering shapes, crackling brush, and the lush feeling of being surrounded by life on all sides. Then start kissing him or her and slowly take of all your clothes. When you are both naked (except for your shoes) leave your clothes behind and continue your walk. Steer it to a quiet place and enjoy yourselves.

For a spicier variation stash the blanket and wine ahead of time. Don't tell your lover where you are going. When you get into the woods, undress only your lover or yourself, then continue your walk with one of you remaining dressed. Leave the clothes behind. The thrill of one being dressed and one naked will send chills up both your spines. By the time you find the blanket you'll probably skip the wine.

The Firecracker Orgasm

Firecracker orgasms suddenly sweep the body past the last bit of self-control and into complete release. How does this happen? The secret is building the intensity so high that orgasms become spontaneous.

Cunnilingus is a good path to her fireworks. He should give her several orgasms with his tongue and lips, or by masturbating her if she likes that. Then, as soon as she has had a strong climax (which may be her second, third, or fourth orgasm) he should enter her immediately, while she is still in the orgasm's final few seconds. Their goal is to bring her right to another orgasm almost instantly. He should stroke her forcefully as soon as he enters, either rapidly or at a medium pace, whichever she finds most exciting.

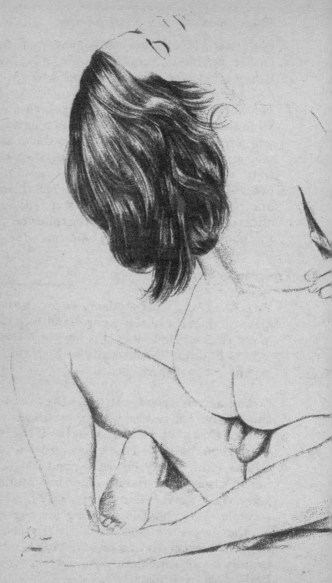

His "technique" is simple: intensify the stimulation when she is already very excited. Massage her nipples, squeeze her buttocks, stimulate her clitoris, or do whatever overloads her senses and propels her into ecstasy. One caution: he should not try this too soon. A woman's excitement builds slower than a man's. With patience, he can bring her to a higher takeoff

level. This helps ensure that she'll go all the way.

Fellatio is a straight road to his fireworks. Her "technique" should parallel the way he overloads her senses. Bring him to a high pitch of excitement, right to the edge of orgasm. Don't stop for a second. Insert him immediately in a position where you both move freely—doggy position, missionary style, etc. Vigorously aim for a huge orgasm—it shouldn't be long in coming.

Encouraging your lover to come is an important part of fireworks. Everything—your words, hips, hands, and mouth—should be urging and stimulating them on. When your lover reaches orgasm, your own probably won't be far behind. The intensity will often prove overwhelming for both of you.

You can produce firecracker orgasms from any point in intercourse. The secret is knowing your lover well enough to recognize when they have reached the trigger point. Enter her or put him inside immediately, making clear that this is the big moment. Go straight for it. Don't be discouraged if it doesn't come off the first time. The distance from take-off to orgasm is infinitesmal, but it may take several tries to learn to cross it quickly.

Natural Sensuousness Is Best

Once you admit that there is much more to your sexuality than having orgasms, you will probably be ready to admit that becoming your full sexual self is a lot more pleasurable than being partly who you are not. You will learn to love enthusiastically because you can do everything you really want.

Sharing and sensitivity will mean more. Words and roles will mean less. When you are eager to love there isn't any need to pretend that you are more of a "liberated woman" or "real man" than the vulnerable and sensitive person you really are. There will be moments when you will be uptight and times when everything goes like Niagara Falls. Whether you are "on" or "off" you'll be really there for your lover, and he or she will be fully there for you. Making love will be more fun than ever before. Affection, excitement, and understanding merge into expanded sensitivity to each other. You will become closer as all your desires become part of your loving.

Turn Loose Your Fire

The words of temperature describe love: love is hot and passionate, frigid and cold, warming, or cooling. These are good descriptions because they reflect the way people feel.

There are other descriptions which aren't as

good. One common misconception is that men are hot and quickly aroused while women are cooler. The implication is that women are less in touch with their sexuality. This misconception was once true. Women's sexual desires used to be caged by the fear of pregnancy and social, economic, and male-enforced roles. Since the quadruple developments of birth control, legal abortion, easy divorce, and women's liberation—developments that appear intimately linked—more women admit the full heat of their sexual desires. Fingertips are probing the old darkness, hands are exploring, and deep pleasures burn away the double standard that cloaked many generations.

Many women have now released their trapped energies and turned them toward all areas of their lives, including sexual maturity. From the former protective coolness, today's attitude is often a renewed search for emotional and physical satisfaction. It has become accepted that almost everyone, regardless of their sex, yearns for relationships that give them more of all that they need. As this is achieved, society is the winner. It begins to possess more of the honest freedom it proclaims as its ideal.

Accept Yourself Fully

Sexual pleasure is strengthened by belief in yourself. Men and women don't bring just their genitals to bed, they bring everything they have been and want to become. If sex were only two humping bodies, people could do anything to anyone, anytime. Many people try this—and eventually discover that it produces emptiness, not pleasure, no matter how intense their orgasmic fire. The more you are yourself in bed—the more you admit your loneliness, sensitivity, and your sexual needs—the more openly you can enjoy ecstasy, transmuting your social persona into total sensuousness.

Bring yourself means reducing the expectations you hold for yourself and your lover. When sex is tied to your self-image it is often made into an "acceptable" ritual. Your chance to scale the heights is diminished. Let go of expectations. Don't let your self-image get in the way. You and your lover may make tonight different from what it has ever been before. If you forget about your limitations and accept yourself fully, it will probably turn out better than you imagine. It can only head upward from there.

Enter Each Other's Private Worlds

The impersonal roles that are common in big cities limit genuine expression. "Apathy" is maligned, yet it may be a successful adjustment to a society that often seems hostile toward the non-apathetic. A secure personal territory is as important as a home of one's own. When this territory is trespassed, defenses are used to preserve whatever integrity remains.

Personal life is just the opposite. The essence of friendship and love is the desire to be open and trusting, to support each other, to share intensely personal moments. In lovemaking this goes much deeper. An actual "individuality of two" is the goal. When it is fully reached, it is an explosive experience.

How is a combined emotional and physical explosion created? Two lovers begin by entering each other's private worlds with tenderness . . . with a touch that says more than a touch . . . appreciating each other's deepest beauties . . . feeling the intensity of shared closeness . . . exploring each other's willingness to surrender to sensuality . . . kindling the spark of passion . . . giving their bodies to each other . . . fusing two into one.

Words cannot sum this up. They do not name the mystery because it cannot be pinned down. Midst an impersonal society, the mystery of love's explosive fusion will always remain.

Experience Multiple Levels of Pleasure

Explosive lovemaking's most extraordinary sensations are produced by the mystery of suddenly becoming more than just yourself. Multiple levels of pleasure spring to life. Animal lust is there, the rejoicing of the primitive beast. Ballet parallels it: graceful coupling burns within the primitive motions. A bond of spirit forms. The universe is silenced by a speechless but triumphant shout. Feelings of being lost in ecstasy but found within oneself play against each other. Intensity builds, yet it is sometimes broken by laughter, teasing, or uncontrollable giggling. Effortless concentration grows as orgasm is approached. Sensuality suddenly expands to its widest, then soars to a new realm, making the impossible real. Afterward, a feeling of lightness, almost of flying, may mingle with exhaustion. The final expression of the experience may be one kiss, the same act but a different feeling from the first kiss that began the fusion.

Every minute acquires texture, depth, and richness through love. The world is concentrated, magnified. Intensity brings transcendence within reach. Passionate lovers overwhelm each other with their beauty, without thought of physical appearance. Their movements convey an incomparable force of reality. The mystery grows and becomes a source of many pleasures.

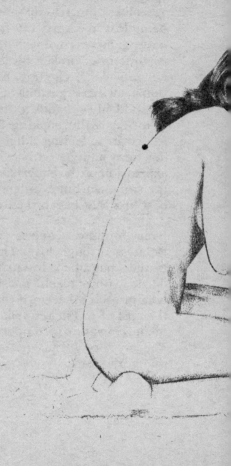

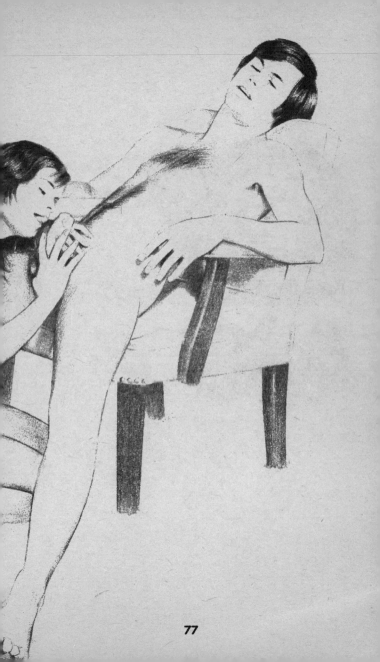

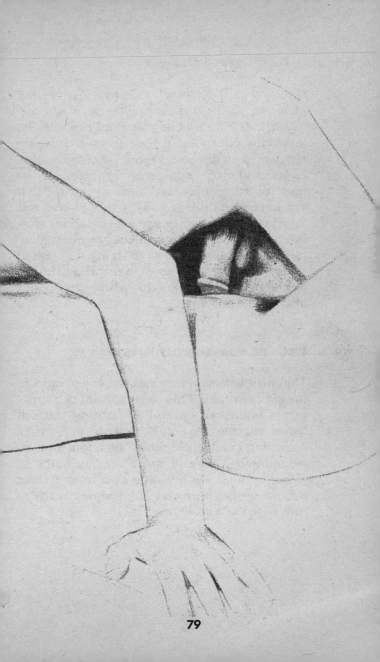

Sensuous Touching and Massage

One way to learn to give and receive deeper pleasures is by massaging each other frequently. Gentle touches such as running the fingertips lightly over your lover's body, interspersed with massaging their muscles, joints, and erogenous areas, are perhaps the most relaxing presexual turn on possible. If you have a vibrator it adds to these massages. Touching and massage are also delicious after intercourse. It is an excellent icebreaker between new lovers. It is so relaxing that sexual release becomes the most natural act in the world, even for people with whom sex doesn't always feel natural.

Warm, Wet, and Unashamedly Responsive

The spirit behind the eyes is one key to unlocking explosive sex. This most special of all moments is created carefully. Turning yourself loose, sharing the most private of worlds, drowning in multiple sensations, touching affectionately . . . and more . . . combine to close the distance between two lovers. Once this bridge has been crossed, they are ready to fuse with each other.

Moving as Gracefully as Gazelles

Pure sensuality. It's a lush and heady experience, a culmination of years of becoming, an invitation to years of happiness. The word foreplay does not describe it, for it implies that touching is a prelude to another act. Sensuality is the goal of itself. Every touch is meaningful.

He kneels over her. His tongue slides effortlessly along her lip, then his cheek rubs against hers as he bends down to kiss her neck. Her back arches. She rises to her elbows and rubs her breasts against his body, her fingers digging into the sheets. He runs his tongue around her ear, inhaling the perfume of her hair. She wraps one arm around his waist and pulls him down, pressing his hips against hers. He rolls them to their side and slithers up the bed, bending forward, kissing his way down her shoulder and then her back. She licks her way

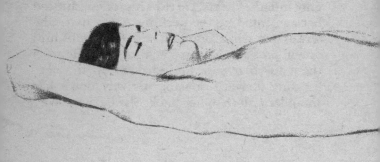

down his stomach as he bends completely around her, his tongue reaching her lower back. They pause for a moment while her tongue and lips caress him, then he starts kissing farther down and appears between her legs. Laughing with joy she bends forward and nuzzles the back of his head as his tongue plays over her lower belly. He rolls on his side. Her upper thigh forms a pillow for his head. They look at each other, smiling, their eyes twinkling. Suddenly, a knot grips their bellies. Their smile turns to a quivering longing. They meet at the same moment, mouths open, their tongues tasting the passionate gifts they eagerly bring to each other.

The New Orality

How good is deeply felt oral sex? A genital kiss can come from the heart. The whole body of the giver vibrates with passion. This ritual is so sensual that the only regret is that it must come to an end—the ecstasy is too much to bear—it drives the recipient over the brink into orgasm, into such intense pleasure that the giver can go into her or his own ecstasy at the same moment. The orgasmic juices flow freely. The tongue and lips give no quarter. Probing onward, they create greater heights of release, forcing uninhibited cries, filling the room with the music of passion.

Deeply felt oral love is a magic carpet to explosive sexuality. It can produce some of the most intense sensations possible, and two lovers who know each other's bodies intimately can share an ultimate union. Before intercourse a woman can let go—and climax several times. A man can usually stand it for only a few minutes, so intense is the pleasure. After intercourse it can be used to revive an orgasm-shattered man. Then, a mutual genital kiss can go on for an hour, soft music playing, two dreamers lost in their caress, finding themselves in the throes of passion from each other's kiss.

Popsicles and Sundaes

The genitals can be the central ingredient in a super dessert, which you can eat with gusto. This is particularly edible when one lover has some qualms about performing cunnilingus or fellatio. The penis or vagina can be topped with chocolate syrup, honey, peanut butter, whipped cream, or other sweet and gooey foods.

Put a towel on the bed before you indulge in this kind of a meal. Whether you have qualms or not, once you try it just for kicks, you may find it so much fun that you start eating these snacks regularly—perhaps daily, as a bedtime treat.

Longer Is Better!

In sex, the most important length is the time that pleasure is extended. There is no question that rapid thrusting movements may bring both a woman and man to orgasm quickly. At the right moment, speed is all that is desired

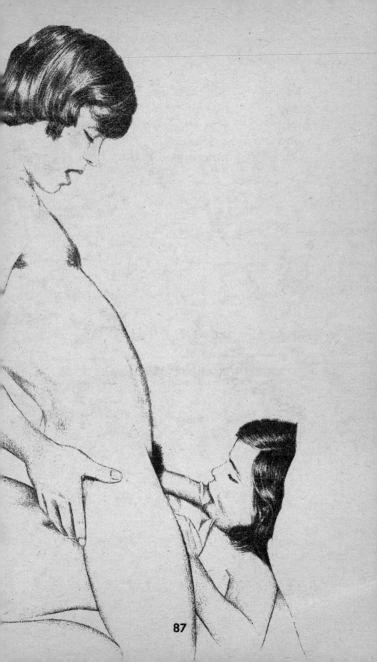

and this intensity is the essence of intercourse. Before that moment is reached, however, the goal should be to build the stimulation as high as it will go, and to extend this period of excitement for a considerable length of time. Long preparation before the climax will increase the quality of the grand finale.

The Purity of Wildness

Making it slow produces the same change as fast, intense lovemaking: with total release comes wildness. Everything disappears but physical and emotional fusion. What is it like?

It was late and they were sleepy when they went to bed. He rolled over and kissed her sensuously good night. She didn't want him to stop and he could tell. Soon he started kissing her neck and shoulders for what seemed like hours. He pulled her nightgown down to her waist and tenderly licked her breasts, sucking the nipples long past their first hardness. She started moaning softly. He kept this up for a long time and she started to writhe sensuously against him. She wanted him right away and reached down to put him inside her, but he slid down under the sheets. He started kissing her feet to her knees. She couldn't lie still. She reached down to rub herself and found she was soaked.

He licked and kissed his way upward slowly. He finally reached her vagina and she instantly had a gigantic orgasm. He kept up and there soon followed a string of orgasms, at least half a dozen of them. Finally, he took his underwear off. He entered, stroked her very, very slowly and she wanted him to go on forever. She came again and again, and gradually he drove her completely wild. Her hips took on a life of their own and started churning furiously. She grabbed his rump and dug her nails in, trying to push his entire body inside. Suddenly he let go and joined her in wildness. "That's right . . . ohhhh . . . come! come!" she moaned. She had the biggest orgasm of all when he came. Their cries must have awakened half the apartment building. By going slowly they built much higher than if they had made it quickly before going to sleep.

As a variation, if you are going slow and your lover is so hot he or she can't stand it, untangle yourself and kneel on the bed next to them. Strip slowly. Make sure your lover watches closely. Return passionately. Your lover will be nearly gone.

By making it slow and discovering the purity of wildness, many more women and men can enjoy more total orgasms.

The Love Roll

Another way to mellow out sex while increasing its pleasure is the love roll. A woman can develop control over her internal vaginal muscles, opening and squeezing them, rolling them, doing this rhythmically in time with the mounting excitement in her man. He can lie on his back or on his side. A moist or lubricated vagina works best. He should not be too excited so that his penis is semi-erect and does not resist her internal muscular contractions.

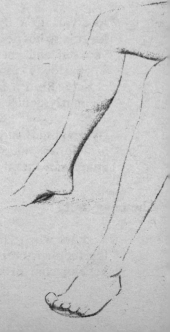

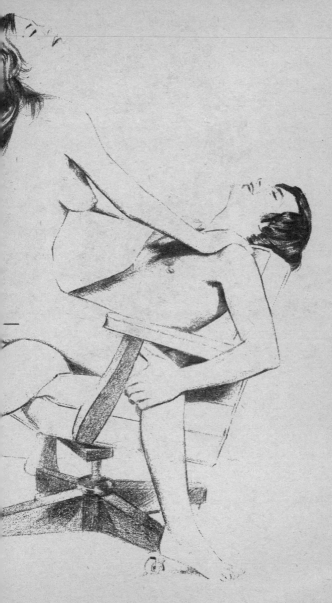

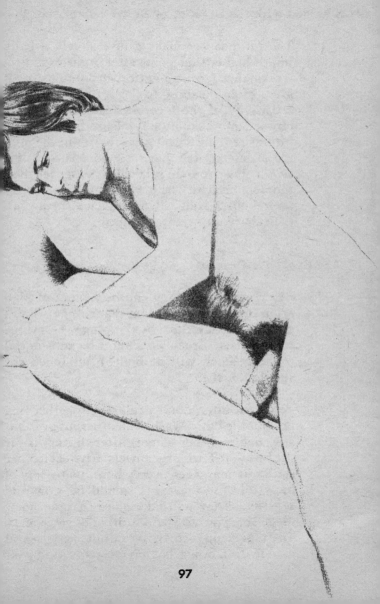

Charged with the Urgency of Now . . . and Now!

The intimacy of making love slowly usually builds higher than going after orgasms or fireworks through straightforward intensity. It gives more meaning to the act of loving. The sensitivity of the lovers to each other is increased. More emotion is released. Fewer inhibitions remain. Two lovers realize in the middle of intercourse that their goal is complete union. They remain relaxed, at ease, yet their moment arrives. The purity of wildness seizes their bodies and will not release them until they share an explosive orgasm.

The Explosive Orgasm

Explosive lovemaking can be a work of high art, a total transformation that comes in a full day of intimacy. Start by skipping sex for three to four days. Breakfast should be substantial because lunch will be light. After lunch she should douche.

Begin the afternoon by relaxing together in a hot bubble bath. Wash each other all over but stop before either comes. After drying, cover the bed with four large towels. Give each other sensuous massages everywhere, using lots of baby oil. The massages should be slow and sensitive. They will take more than an hour. Make sure you stop before either of you comes. Then spend up to forty-five minutes giving oral love to each other, having intercourse in your favorite positions, and sixty-nine—always stopping before either of you has an orgasm. Then rest for about five to ten minutes. Having come so close to orgasm so many times, you are unbelievably ready for the afternoon climax.

If you enjoy anal intercourse, do the following: put a pillow in the middle of the bed. He lies on his back with the pillow under his hips. She then lies on top of him, also on her back. She puts six Ben-Wa balls into her vagina. They stay in because her vagina is tilted slightly upwards. She then twists the upper half of her body so they can kiss. While she is inserting the Ben-Wa balls he should touch her sensually. After the Ben-Wa balls are inserted and they are kissing, he massages her nipples with one hand and her clitoris with the other. In about five minutes, or when they are aroused, he inserts his still oiled penis into her anus. (If her anus is not oily from the massage it should be lubricated before beginning.) Once he is inside they should start kissing again and he should return his hands to her breasts and clitoris. Now two horny and excited lovers are in total embrace: mouth, breast, clitoris, vagina, and anus are all receiving stimulation at once. Don't hold back any longer. She will probably go into a state of nearly continuous orgasm that will last as long as he lasts. She might even pass out in delirium. When he has come they roll over on their sides and fall asleep for about an hour.

If you do not enjoy anal intercourse, you can use any rear entry position where he can give vaginal, clitoral, and breast stimulation at the same time. She can give herself the clitoral stimulation, if she wants.

After waking remove the Ben-Wa balls and have vaginal intercourse in your favorite positions. Your sexual appetite will remain strong because the bath, massage, and unconsummated intercourse kept approaching orgasm but always stopped short. After intercourse, shower and dress then go out for dinner and the evening. Make love once more before going to sleep, this time slowly with lots of oral love and sensuous moving against each other. Enjoy a quickie in the morning. This is a nice finish to an ecstatic experience.

The whole day combines to take you "all the way" to all kinds of pleasures and satisfaction. Two lovers should feel very close afterward. They've shared everything with each other.

The Search for the Ultimate Orgasm

Is an explosive orgasm real? Is it an impossible journey by an improbable crew in search of an elusive creature that doesn't exist? No it isn't, no more than the female orgasm for a woman who has never experienced one.

Expanding your sexuality is complex because it takes two people who are reaching out individually yet are trying to grow together. Success depends on both of you—and on the quality of your relationship. Together you can make today depressing or simply nothing, a day that is lost forever. Or you can make it a superday, a day to remember for the rest of your life.

If two lovers are willing to have patience and try, they can learn to make time stand still. Sensuality, passion and ecstasy can be their familiar friends. An ultimate orgasm—and an ultimate union together—are within the realm of possibility.

Making It Slow

Climbing the mountain quickly, with fire and intensity, is not the only way to the top. Explosive sex, in fact, is often more accessible when you go slow—and build higher. When ecstasy is prolonged the whole body starts to vibrate. If it is kept up it starts to feel like you've been having continuous orgasms for hours.

It is delicious spending the whole evening listening to music and loving very, very slowly. This kind of evening is different. It is not bang, bang, climax, over, then doing it again. You can make love for a while then stop and smoke a cigarette, change the record, have a drink, give a massage, or talk. After each interlude you can make love and maybe come or maybe not, but just go on for hours, growing closer throughout the evening. When you finally finish it feels as though you've become part of each other, perhaps closer than you've ever been before.

The "Intensity of Orgasm" Cycle

There is a difference in the intensity with which a man and a woman sexually respond at any given moment. A man's sexual interest is subject to irregular variations. Some factors that may affect it are the length of time since his last orgasm, his available energy, and his general state of health. Similar conditions also affect a woman, but the intensity of her orgasms also rise and fall with her menstrual cycle and the different hormones that it produces.

Estrogen is the hormone that stimulates her sexual excitement. A woman's glands begin releasing estrogen into her bloodstream at about the middle of the menstrual flow. The amount of estrogen released climbs steadily until ovulation, about thirteen to fourteen days later.

Estrogen is a stimulant and during this period a woman is increasingly sensitized to sexual pleasure. It is as if nature's invisible hand were at work, not only providing an egg for fertilization but enticing a woman through sexual pleasure to be most eager for impregnation at precisely the moment that it is most likely to occur. A woman can experience orgasms of considerable intensity during the latter days of the first half of her menstrual cycle.

Once ovulation occurs the production of estrogen decreases. In addition, a second hormone is produced for the first time. This is progesterone and it has a sedative influence. It inhibits somewhat the sexual excitement, though overall sexual responsiveness can remain at a high level. Progesterone produces increased feelings of tenderness and motherhood, which may change the character of her desires from passion to gentle loving. Progesterone is released into the bloodstream from approximately the fourteenth day until the twenty-eighth day of her cycle. It continues until the unfertilized egg dies and the menstrual flow begins once again. During this time a woman's orgasms may be milder, or she might not have orgasms at all.

Just before ovulation a woman's sexual response is heightened and after ovulation it may not be as passionate in its intensity. This does not mean that sexual pleasure cannot be as much fun or as meaningful. The vigor of the response is not the only determinant of sexual satisfaction. Some women have orgasms throughout their entire monthly cycle, even during the beginning of their period when the production of both hormones has ceased temporarily. For other women, the diminished capacity to have an orgasm does not mean that sex is less important. In fact, it may be more important since his loving reassures her that she is just as desirable and attractive even though her passions are not as intense.

Her orgasmic capacity can be increased if a couple feels this is important, though this should not be necessary. The tenderness and quality of lovemaking are more important than the size and frequency of her orgasms. If a couple works toward improving their tenderness and responsiveness to each other, her orgasms may increase in frequency and intensity over a long period of time. It is important to understand this "intensity of orgasm" cycle because orgasmic expectations that are unrealistically high can produce disappointment when what is happening is a release of progesterone that is completely normal. They both need to know that she can sometimes go crazy with pleasure and at other times prefer slow and gentle loving with no orgasm at all.

The Prison of Good Technique

The development of satisfying loving is never finished. Sex is a delicate process and it is intimately connected with the mood and attitude of each lover every time they give themselves to each other. Techniques that previously proved successful may require further experimentation, improvisation, and elaboration.

No standardized procedure is enough, even if it is developed over years of affectionate loving. An often repeated technique may lead to a lack of responsiveness that can diminish sexual spontaneity and the fulfillment loving provides.

Every time they go to bed a couple must work out the approaches and responses that they feel are most appropriate at that moment. To the extent that they standardize their patterns, they fail to express the sincere and natural feelings they could discover in their loving. These patterns may even prove inhibiting and prevent the further development of deeper physical and emotional satisfactions.

Good sex requires constant improvisation. Since judgment is involved, this will not always be accurate. It will nevertheless be more accurate than frequent repetition of the same or similar patterns. In addition, the couple can explore each other and themselves with greater freedom.

Over a period of years, this hightened responsiveness can produce some startling changes. A couple may come to possess a much more varied repertoire after they have been lovers for years than earlier. In fact, what they considered wrong during the development of their relationship may seem right later on, and their early restraint may turn out to appear wrong.

There is an unreachable though worthwhile ideal implied. A couple has the chance to develop a profound understanding of each other's reactions so that each responds to the other's needs without hesitation. Once loving becomes spontaneous, creative, and tender, it expresses the immediate desires of the couple. It varies according to the sensitivities and needs of each partner each time they go to bed together. In the end, love always comes before technique.

No Thyself?

Sexual inhibitions have varying degrees of strength. They are rooted in either personal psychological experiences or they are cultural and therefore common. What is a cultural inhibition? one that produces many difficulties is the silent treatment that sex gets in a large number of marriages, even though both partners may be relatively passionate and uninhibited in their lovemaking. The quiet way these couples attempt sexual experimentation when open and frank discussions would accelerate their growth clearly expresses the kind of influence culture still has on many apparently free and self-accepting people.

Many kinds of psychological, emotional, and cultural factors reduce the ability to feel or enjoy sexual pleasure. What are some of them? Childhood or early adolescent experiences of masturbation or heterosexual love can sometimes produce a sense of guilt or shame. Sexual fears may be produced when young children or adolescents are severely punished for quite natural sexual investigations. Many churches still link sex and sin. In some adolescents, years of unconsummated heavy petting may condition a "no" response to their sexual drive, making it difficult for them to let go once they are married. One powerful cause is an unhappy childhood in a home that is sexually starved and devoid of affection. Equally stifling is an identification with a mother or father who has been deeply hurt by their mate. Fear of pregnancy may produce a lack of sexual response. This is a very constrictive fear since pregnancy when a woman is not ready for it is a traumatic experience. The fear of pregnancy can cause great anxieties.

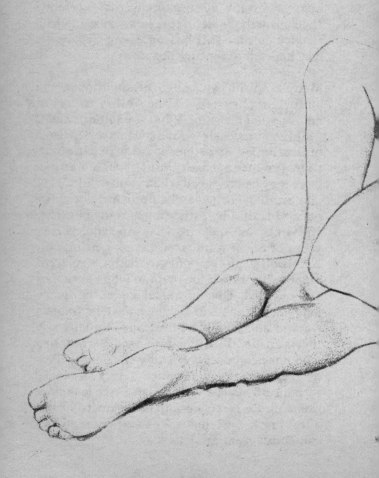

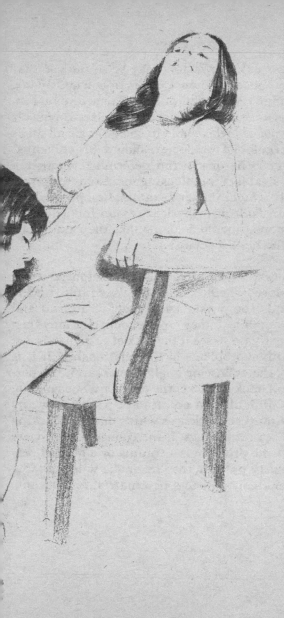

These or other factors may be so intense that they cause impotence in a man or frigidity in a woman. Where this or a diminished sexual response exists, it is generally wise to consult specialists who can help solve the problem. A gynecologist or doctor should be consulted first, so he or she can determine whether a physical factor is blocking the sexual response. Only when a doctor's examination proves that there isn't any physical reason for a lack of response should a couple take their questions to the next specialist.

This should be a marriage counselor, who will explore whether or not this couple understands the physiological facts of arousal and intercourse. If they do, the counselor may then investigate to see if the lack of response is due to other problems in the relationship. If it is not, the counselor might then search the personal background of the partner who is having the difficulty, in an attempt to discover any traumatic experiences which may be blocking the sexual feelings. If the counselor discovers that the problem is a trauma or a fixated personality pattern, then he or she will probably refer the couple to a psychiatrist for therapy.

Almost all people who have sexual inhibitions can be helped to achieve a satisfying sexual relationship. The gynecological, marriage counseling, and psychiatric literature is filled with cases of all kinds of people who have been helped with all kinds of problems. Sexual pleasure is not always or even usually automatic. It is a fact that the more you learn and the more experienced you become, the more pleasure you can feel. If an individual has a problem he or she cannot handle alone or with their mate, they should not feel embarrassed to seek the help that they need. There simply isn't any reason to resign yourself to living with an inhibited sexual response when professional help is available.

"Oh, no. The opposite is true."

Reflex conditioning begins in childhood. By the time a person reaches adulthood the contemplation of a particular sex act, such as oral intercourse, may be enough to trigger a strong negative response in them. This response might be a bitter condemnation of the partner who suggests the activity. Or, it might be nausea, diarrhea or constipation.

This strong a response is clear evidence that the affected individual's deepest reaction is positive, not negative. A strong reaction is produced psychologically by a psychic blockage or suppression of an initial physical desire. In truth, he or she is not saying, "You're disgusting for suggesting that," but, "I feel sick because I want to do that."

Maximum "Wow!"

Satisfying each other in three or four ways isn't enough. Half a dozen ways are just a start. To have a full palette of colors to paint their pleasures, a couple needs to discover a variety of ways they both enjoy making love. There is simply no substitute for this kind of variety if they want their sexuality to give them maximum numbers of "Wow!"

In a way, this is a performance standard, but it is a very broad one that is based on self-knowledge and an affectionate relationship. You are not expected to expand your sexuality more than you want. What you are expected to do is to understand a wide variety of ways to give each other pleasure—slow, intense, gentle, rough, quick, lingering, etc.—so that you look forward to sex, simply because you can always give each other what you need. This isn't a high performance extreme. It is a well developed ability to give and receive sexual pleasure with the person you love.

The Psychosexual Balance

Psychological moods affect sexual functioning. Thought, memory, attitude, and personality affect genital and emotional reactions in both men and women. Sex is simply much bigger than the physical body. Conflicts over money, religion, feelings of hostility because of neglect or even a single discourtesy may diminish sexual pleasure. Nothing damages the sexual side of a relationship more than a continuing failure to come to terms with each other in some other area of the relationship. This is why sexual adjustment sometimes appears difficult to achieve. The problem is not in the sexual responses of one or the other partner. It is in one or several other areas of the relationship.

Generally, if a couple has developed a satisfactory cooperative approach to solving the problems they face in their relationship, they will not experience many difficulties in coming together sexually. They share the knowledge that whatever their problems, they will be able to resolve them satisfactorily, so these will usually not interfere with the physical expression of their love for one another.

The sexual relationship may be used as a barometer of the degree to which companionship and trust have been established. Low sexual adjustment will often parallel very little happiness. People who are very happy seldom have poor sex lives. Sexual love is an important part of the total pattern of affection and rapport a person shares with their mate. If their overall pattern is a satisfying one, sex will usually be satisfying. If there are problems in the larger relationship, these will be mirrored in its physical contacts.

Some sense of emotional dependence, deep commitment, or mutuality should be shared by a couple because this promotes a more fulfilling sexual relationship. When a couple has married for egotistical reasons, is compulsively selfish, or uses marriage to satisfy a need such as excessive dependency or marrying for money, this couple will usually pay the price of its lack of open sincerity sexually. They will not possess the essential element of sharing and mutual surrender. If a couple cannot share sincerely outside the bedroom, they will not come to possess much of each other's bodies either. The lack of a solid foundation to their relationship will block a fully developed sexual compatibility. While a few couples do manage to find sexual pleasure even though they have basically unhappy marriages, this is not the typical case.

Good sex is an important source of emotional strength and commitment in a relationship. It builds a reservoir of closeness on which a couple can draw when they must resolve other strains in their relationship. The sex can also give them a vehicle for releasing their other stresses, and actually provide a healing action.

When there is an argument or a problem, if there is also a good sexual relationship, this may reassure the couple that they have some way in which to reach out to each other in spite of their differences, and give them a way to rebuild their affection. The healing action of deep intimacy brings them back together and gives them a renewed mutual interest in solving their problems.

What Can You See by the Dawn's Early Light?

During the years that a couple shares the same bedroom, the first few minutes after waking set the tone for the day's relationship. This time also re-establishes the quality of the relationship that the couple shares. Another few minutes that are equally important are when they arrive home after work, just before dinner. These few minutes at these two times of the day reveal the quality of their relationship more accurately than most people realize.

This is a bit complex, because the morning's first few minutes are much more than a routine to "get up and get going." Below the level of waking awareness—which can often be dull and foggy—couples bombard each other with messages and signals. Moods and attitudes are being sent out, and impressions are being received. These impressions influence the day's work and activities. They can determine whether you smile at your boss or are sullen all

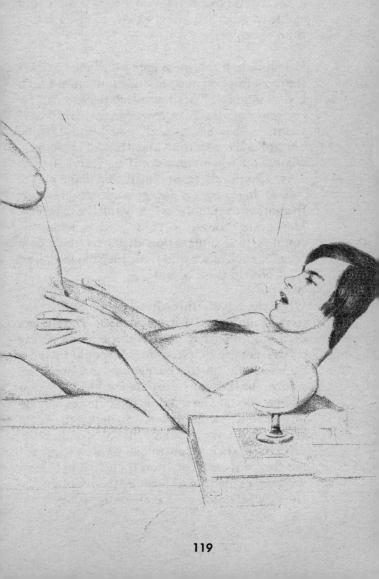

day. They can also determine whether that night will be spent in loving or in evasion. And summed together, they set the tone for a lifetime of relating.

Probably half the messages—and many times the most important ones—are sent out through body language. These nonverbal signs can reinforce or contradict the words you say. If he is silent, makes short and sharp movements, crumples his pajamas and throws them on a chair, and when she asks if he feels all right says, "Don't talk to me until I've had a cup of coffee," his overall message is startlingly clear. In another couple she might yank the covers off him even though it is a cold morning. A couple's first interaction discloses their concern for each other and their idea of what their relationship is all about.

When there is an unresolved problem it is easy to start the day with an argument. The subject of the argument can be the temperature setting on the electric blanket, how he could be more "timesaving" in his bathroom and breakfast routine, or the way he orders the kind of breakfast he wants. These kinds of arguments magnify a couple's differences, and never give them a chance to tackle their problems directly. They build their resentments so high they cannot confront each other on their real problems without exploding. These patterns often become predictable and eventually destructive.

Since people usually start the day with fairly habitual patterns, it is important to consciously choose patterns that yield satisfaction and closeness instead of unhappiness, frustration, or loneliness. Concern for your partner and his or her feelings can be shown in a wide variety of ways, all of which communicate the interest, appreciation, or affection that can produce positive by-products all day long.

Some couples intertwine upon awakening. Others smile and say, "Hello, sweetheart." There can be a soft conversation about the day's coming activities, a shared morning breath of air at an open window, a hug or caress, or just a simple mood of sharing the morning routine and helping each other through it. These kinds of contact set a rewarding pace and attitude for the hours that follow. They clearly symbolize the kind of relationship that both partners can enjoy.

Think about what you are doing. The morning's opening minutes can be very satisfying. Take your mate in your arms and whisper, "I love you." Kiss them on the forehead or cheek, and add a caress in a place that arouses them but not so sensitive that it jars them. Or bend over them tenderly, rub the back of his or her neck, and whisper, "It's time for another beautiful day, lover."

The way you wake up together describes the

quality of your relationship. Do you use love, tenderness, and gentle humor, or thoughtlessness, masked hostility, or outright anger? Try discussing this and asking each other how you would like to wake up together. This simple conversation might give you new ways to re-establish a warm relationship each morning. This can pay off in a new intimacy and closeness that may help the whole relationship become happier.

Affectionate Evening or Lonely Twilight?

The first few minutes when a couple greets each other after work are just as important as the first moments of morning. Not only does this pre-dinner encounter reveal as much about the quality of a relationship as waking up, but it has a powerful impact on the emotional quality of the evening hours that follow.

Many couples have traditional patterns. He walks in complaining about the traffic, the cold or rainy weather, how tired he is, or his problems down at the office. In another home everyone might be instructed not to talk to "dad" until he has had two or three martinis. A woman may mirror these lonely tendencies, particularly if she has just returned from her own job and must prepare dinner and attend to the kids at the same time. Or, if she doesn't work, she might start complaining about her problems immediately. The children were bad and he has to spank Tommy right away. The groceries are too expensive, her housework was tiring that day, or she's been hassled by a thoughtless relative.

In a different home both partners might go a tiny bit out of their way to be attractive and nice for each other when they greet each other in the evening. He might comb his hair, wash his face, and put on some cologne to freshen up just before leaving the office. Then he might arrive smiling cheerfully, and give his wife and kids a warm hello. She might also take a few minutes to freshen up, or dab on a bit of perfume.

Children sense these attitudes and they are affected by what goes on between their mother and father. If a couple greets each other with a smile, a kiss, and a few minutes of playful or peaceful affection, their children will feel much better about the coming family togetherness at dinner than if their parents are irritated and curt with each other. In the family of the more distant couple, there is a greater chance that during dinner their kids will be indifferent or aggravating.

These first few minutes affect the couple's relationship for hours. If one of them is upset he or she might use the first minutes to dump their problems or irritations on the other's shoulders. As soon as this unloading is over, he or she might think that they feel better, but this has done more harm than good. A few minutes of unrelieved verbal static will usually turn someone off for hours, particularly when this is a symbol that the troubled person cannot be counted on for good feelings and warmth whenever they imagine they have problems.

The Fatigue Factor

One increasingly common obstacle to frequent good sex is the lack of enough physical and psychic energy for maintaining a sexual relationship. Fatigue is one of the biggest enemies of sexual pleasure. The struggle for position, career success, and wealth is fierce and demanding. Many men and now many more women are investing so much of their energy in this struggle that they do not have a reserve left for coitus.

Both men and women suffer a lack of potency when they are over-worked or tired. Career goals cause stress as well as a depletion of strength. The stress puts an additional drain on the available emotional energy. This problem is easily overcome, if an individual or a couple wants to solve it. They must budget enough energy and time for their sexual rela-

tions. Once they try it and see how much vitality good loving brings, they will realize that this part of their life is central to what they are all about and not just an afterthought.

In a happier home this first encounter can give a loving couple the chance to renew their feelings for each other. If they take the time to pay full attention to each other, even for a few minutes, it brings them back together as a man and a woman. Conversation is not as important as feelings of closeness. Tuning in to each other does not mean questions of how they are feeling or how the day went. Observations such as, "You look like you had an okay day today," or, "You look a little tired today," tell your mate you care and want to be involved in their feelings. This suggests a willingness to listen with your heart, and to help if you are needed, without prying into irrelevant details.

This attention is an important part of these minutes, but it isn't all. Either a lingering kiss or some physical contact helps bring you back together. Hold hands, put your arms around each other, touch an arm or cheek gently, or do whatever caressing give both of you a feeling of affection. Take the time to relax before you add any pressures. Look forward to these few moments. They can bring more than warmth for later hours. They will probably prove very pleasurable in and of themselves.

Dressing for Your Lover

Tight clothes or costumes turn many people on. If she likes the shape of your buttocks, wear tight jeans for her. She can do the same, if you want her to. In tight pants you both appear practically naked to each other. Tight clothes also add friction to movement. If you go out together dressed like this, you might have to rush home early to make love.

Dress to suit your imagination or fantasies around the house. Very brief, thin underwear look good on both men and women. The old style black stockings are enjoying a new popularity. Create imaginative "costumes." She might combine dark stockings, high heeled shoes or sandals, a very short skirt, and remain nude from the waist up except for a natural looking necklace or choker. He might walk out of the bathroom naked, grab a scarf and tie it in a band around his head, start snarling and jumping, calling himself a rapacious 18th century pirate—and jump on you!

To the Sexual Victors Go the Orgasms of Old Age

Those who develop active and satisfying sex lives in youth and middle age can usually look forward to far less sexual stress and much better loving in old age. Everyone encounters a sexual decline after the age of forty. This decline is gradual, however, and at no point is there a sudden diminishing of sexual desire.

A woman's menopause, known as the change of life, occurs in most women between the ages of forty-five and fifty. The breasts gradually shrink, the abdomen gains some weight, the voice may deepen, and some hair may grow on the chin and neck. A general nervousness and irritability may be brought on by these changes.

A similar but less well defined change occurs in men at a slightly older age. A man may even experience a temporary loss of virility and fertility, with some men having prostrate gland complications. Men who have been sexually active throughout their lives may feel disturbed. A few men will resort to an affair to attempt to compensate for the threat they feel to their manhood.

These are natural changes in both men and women and there isn't any reason to discontinue sexual activity during them. In fact, satisfying sexual intercourse and the experience of orgasm during these periods both restores confidence and helps relax the anxieties that these physical changes create. It has been established that sexual desire and sexual satisfaction generally continue on about the same level after these physical changes are over.

Neither female menopause nor the male change ends a couple's lovemaking despite a common stereotype that says this is the end. The man and the woman who accept and use their sexual potentials throughout their lives will experience less stress during these years. They will generally emerge with many years of loving to look forward to. It is as though they are being rewarded in their old age for having loved so much and so well when they were younger.

The First Five Minutes in Bed with a New Lover

Those who are just beginning relationships need to use some of the same approaches as longtime lovers. But they also need extra empathy or sensitivity to help overcome the apprehensions which might flaw the harmony that lovers try to establish.

A sexual encounter often begins with very little preface. People who are experienced in giving love tenderly and with understanding will often do well in these situations. They aim directly for genuine, not quick, satisfaction and fulfillment. In those who have or encounter hangups, it is especially important to fill the first few minutes with warmth and mutual appreciation. Those individuals who have sex almost without learning each other's names do not need to learn anything about the first minutes in bed. They already know exactly what they want.

The first five minutes of a sexual encounter begin before a couple is in each other's arms. Contact starts with the eyes instead of the hands or body. Let your partner know how much you enjoy looking at him or her. People respond to visual appreciation. They may return this warmth in the form of a more exciting sexual experience. Watch your mate undress and tell him or her by your reaction how much you like his or her body. For example, he might tell her how stimulating it is to see her completely naked for the first time, or the thrill he feels at the thought of kissing her appealing body. She might tell him how much the sight of his penis fires her sexual desires.

Kissing becomes the next medium of arousal, as well as the first gift of physical pleasure. Most people think that they know how to kiss well, but many a sexual experience has been disrupted by two partners who either kissed with too little feeling or so ardently that one of them felt devoured. Take the time to discover how your partner kisses. Exchange suggestions and impressions with your mouth and tongue. The mouth is a symbolic sex organ at this stage. Gentle lips can release a hidden firmness, a tongue can probe then yield to counterthrusts, teeth can gently bite or nibble, or the tip of the tongue can lick the lips. These kinds of kisses, alone, can create passionate intensity. Sexual excitement can sweep the body in only a few minutes, and all the senses can become awake and alive when two such lovers discover their eagerness to give intense pleasures to each other.

As eyes arouse and kisses whet the appetite, the hands begin to fondle and caress. If these touches are gentle and affectionate, both responding to arousal yet being able to lighten up while searching for higher excitements, touching can establish a bond of unrestrained intimacy between first time lovers. It is sometimes sensuous to touch his or her cheeks while kissing very tenderly, giving your soon-to-be inner companion the message that you are

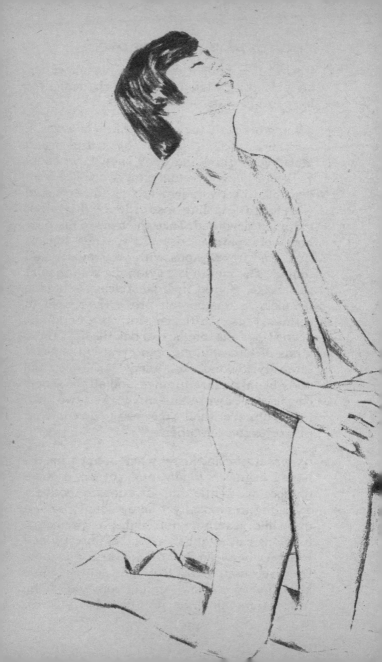

completely open to them inside yourself. Equally sensual touches on the breasts, chest, lower belly, thighs, buttocks, and genital areas can add the message of intense longing. Sex is not automatic, especially when it is very good. It has to be fired with sensitive passions and built carefully, if new lovers are to reach the same ecstatic release as long-time lovers.

As the sensuality builds, awe and deeper affection enter the relationship. This kind of loving can continue for hours, each overwhelming the other with their desire for closeness and their complete acceptance of each other as emotional as well as physical companions. These are the kinds of preliminaries which rapidly open the senses wide and generate the feverish desires necessary for maximum fusion and satisfaction. When this is reached in a first time encounter, it is almost certain that there will be many more of these occasions.

Making a New Love Click

While a few couples discover that they are totally compatible right from the start, this is not that common. It usually takes time to learn about and adjust to each other. This is doubly true in sex, where two people are learning about each other's most private and intimate selves.

A period of sexual experimentation is often necessary before a couple arrives at complete sexual surrender. Depending on the attitudes and experience of the people involved, this may take several weeks, several months, or many years. With frank communication or a marriage counselor (if professional help is needed), this period can be shortened considerably.

In general, one partner will be more experienced than the other. Where they are about equally experienced, each will have preferences of their own. An early period of adjustment is normal. Men and women who are starting out with new partners should remember that there is a natural interval between beginning sexual relations and the achievement of full responsiveness—even when two lovers start with an explosive involvement.

The two biggest obstacles to eventual success are anxiety in the one who is "slower" and impatience by the one who is "faster." In many couples the man is impatient with the woman. She becomes anxious because of his expectations and this further inhibits her responsiveness. He decides that she is partly or wholly frigid, and reduces his affection and attention toward her. She begins to question herself and her capacities. Intercourse becomes less frequent. They eventually start to feel less love for each other. Then they resign themselves to an inadequate sexual relationship or break up altogether.

This pattern occurs in reverse with increasing frequency as women become the sexual aggressors. If she becomes impatient with him, he may question his sexual ability. Self-doubt increases his "performance anxiety." It may even damage his ability to function and leave him temporarily impotent. If this cycle gets out of control it will lead to a mutually disappointing conclusion and probably force the relationship to end.

Neither of these situations is necessary or inevitable. In fact, with simple patience and understanding they could both be avoided. It is true that some sexual relationships will take longer to flower and bear fruit than either lover anticipated, but a gradual development is far better than a poor or strained relationship that ends in resignation and failure.

A Brand New Honeymoon

The wedding and the honeymoon are often felt to be the most momentous and meaningful experiences in life, at least by many women. Yet the wedding memories of many couples are of a frantic social event that was fairly complicated. And the honeymoon that followed may have been a time of early adjustment that came too early in their sexual relationship for them to taste real ecstasy. It is possible to symbolically recreate these days. A new experience of them can be as memorable and significant as the original events.

A wedding is a complex social function. For the couple, it is not really a social event at all. It is the climax of months of growing together in trust and companionship. For them, the personal meaning of this moment stands above everything else.

Years later, a husband and wife who are still in love may repeatedly re-pledge themselves to each other through small gestures such as the look he gives her when he raises his wine glass to her before taking a sip, or the gentle way she straightens his tie in the morning before they both leave for work. They still share a bond, but these subtle vows may not be enough. As a couple settles down in their marriage the early tenderness and ecstasy become more casual. Other values surge into the forefront of attention to conventional responsibilities before marriage, but his view shifts to that of a hus-band who must earn a living and face a lifetime of diminished glamor.

Over the years, their love turns to companionship. The passion that drew them together may recede into the background. As their companionship becomes familiar, sex may express af-

fection instead of love. Intercourse may be quicker and much less intense. The original demonstrations of love may no longer be part of it. This can be revitalized by a new symbolic ceremony, perhaps on a birthday or anniversary. Dinner together, without the children, a little wine or other spirits, and an exchange of new vows can be brought together to create a very special moment. Each partner might write out their own "re-marriage pledge" to the other beforehand, and then read it in a private ceremony before or after the meal, whenever they feel it appropriate.

A new honeymoon is indispensable after this ceremony. The first honeymoon was a time when the couple's adjustments to each other were just beginning. Then, each person's privacy and isolation took the first steps toward shared living, not only sexually, but in every other way. If a couple went on an extensive trip or followed a busy vacation schedule, this may not have given them sufficient time to quietly explore each other's personality. Each person had years of hopes and expectations to resolve and adjust to the specific person they married.

If this adjustment is to be successful, they need to concentrate on each other and on themselves in relation to their new partner.

A brand new honeymoon might be as rewarding as the first honeymoon, perhaps even more so because the adjustment to each other has matured. The new honeymoon should be at least a weekend at a nearby resort, or preferably a full week with plenty of time for each other. Time should be reserved for exploring both new and old attitudes and developing any valuable additions to the relationship that the couple wants. The attitudes of mutuality, tenderness, and patience can be strengthened. New sexual desires can be made the focus of patient and understanding experiments.

This kind of a symbolic wedding and second honeymoon can be powerful experiences. Deep emotions can be reached once again. Both may learn that they still can give and receive sympathetic understanding, sensitive encouragement, and expressions of appreciation. If emotional independence has developed over the years, or if one has grown independent while the other remained dependent, both may rediscover their needs for emotional dependence—and admit that this is a positive source of strength in marriage. Failure to receive emotional support is frustrating, and independence has its price. Rediscovering each other's and their own deep emotional needs may prove very rewarding.

For all its advantages, a new marriage ceremony and a second honeymoon cannot achieve
everything anew. Daily life imposes itself all
too quickly. If a couple develops more affection
and carries this back into their daily lives, this
may be achievement enough.

A Paradox of Good Loving: Adultery!

Someone who enjoys an excellent sexual relationship in marriage is still attracted to outsiders. In fact, the man or woman who enjoys good sex within marriage will be more susceptible to others than those who have been disappointed by the sexual side of marriage.

The only drawback to good married loving is that it is always with the same person. Sheer novelty is a powerful contributor to sexual stimulation. When the marriage is strong and stable, extra-marital adventures are ephemeral. It is a momentary thrill or amusement. The other woman or the other man can be enjoyed physically, without ever considering throwing over the marriage for them. If there is any compulsion involved, it is to return to the arms of the spouse, not to find comfort for long in a different bed.

Total Ecstasy in 200 Minutes a Week?

When the need for immediate ecstasy clashes with tenderness, ecstasy loses gracefully so that it may return spontaneously later on. There cannot be a 30 minute schedule for manufacturing ecstasy. Lovers reach ecstasy when they are ready, and it can be immediately—but it cannot be planned. It arrives when unrestrained physical intensity arrives.

Ecstasy reflects the special feelings lovers bring each other. It is expressed in hands touching and urging, lips opening wide, thighs moving against other thighs, and bodies probing and thrusting against one another. In the stillness that follows, tiny movements encapsulate all meaning: a touch, a smile, a gentle kiss on the lips.

Only one schedule can bring ecstasy immediately: This is the bliss of long-time lovers who share a private highway to a powerful destination. Even this will grow shallow with time, if it is not varied by the sexual renewal an unhurried sharing of each other can bring.

The Expansion of Sexual Fulfillment

Perfection in lovemaking is not won at once, then possessed and automatically enjoyed every day after that. It is an art, not a skill, and it takes years to develop. This is revealed in the way lovers touch each other. It is sensitive. These lovers are aware of what their partner is feeling in lovemaking. They share the desire to heighten that feeling: gently, roughly, slowly, or fast. An inner bond has fused them together.

Every time their art develops a little more it reforges their bond anew.

Take the time to try many kinds of lovemaking. Pass the active and passive roles back and forth freely. Be open and receptive, not skeptical. Introduce new techniques as often as you like, devising your own proportions of old and new ways to love. If you mix coital orgasm with oral, manual, and other ways to produce orgasms, you will probably enjoy more climaxes. Love will be an anticipated adventure, a longed-for activity. It will never again be just a physical release.

Reveling in the Mysteries of Each Other

In spite of the common opinion that some people "have it all together," there is a powerful and vast silence surrounding our noisy society. Two lovers can protect each other from this silence, or enjoy it . . . lie together and feel their closeness . . . say nothing and yet say everything . . . ride the tides of passion that swell to a crest in their bodies, then ebb into the peace, security, and comfort of each other's arms.

There is much more to each person—including ourselves—then we will ever know. Midst a wide variety of human cultures each person must face life in their own way. If there is an individual essence, it is how each person attempts to create happiness—their individual approach to life. The "human condition" that counts isn't the condition of humanity. It is how each person copes with the challenges that arise each day.

This is not a simple mirror. Sometimes despair shakes an individual's world. Other times the heights are within reach. What does each person bring to their despair? To their drive for ecstasy and fulfillment? Multiple trails reach into the past and future from each person, each gesture, each word. The experience of love is much more than sex. It is a human drama with a thousand unanswerable questions, and these mysteries enrich the love two people feel for each other.

Be a Friend, Not a Judge

Many people do not tell their lover what they really desire because they are afraid that the person they love will suddenly become a judge and cease to be an understanding friend. This is a common problem. Start solving it by listening deeply to the one you love. Try to accept what is unknown and unpredictable within them. This helps you see them in more than one or several roles. Your increased tolerance will free you from feeling like you have to put a limit or judgment on their behavior.

The Inner Equality of Lovers

If you want to get all you can out of a relationship, there must be equality and understanding both in and out of bed. Give as much as you take, and vice versa. There is no other way to

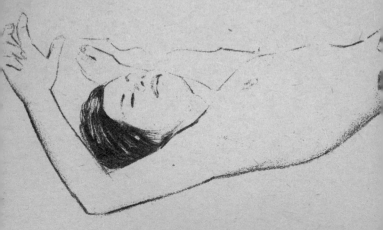

get down with someone and let it *all* out. Too often, Jeff falls in love with Ann's image of himself, taking it to be himself. Then Jeff must not lose Ann, because he would lose himself. What's more, Jeff becomes jealous if any one else's image is reflected in her mirror. And vice versa.

In another relationship, Sue wants Larry to want her. And Larry wants Sue to want him. To get Larry to want her she pretends she wants him. To get Sue to want him he pretends he wants her. Go straight to divorce and do not stop at love.

Equality and understanding can be an alternative: Steve wants Diane to be herself and Diane wants Steve to be himself. Steve and Diane both understand this. They also tell each other that they know, so that they both know that they know. They have the chance to find love because they have the freedom to give and take what they really feel. When they make love it is sometimes his trip, sometimes hers, but always theirs.

Sex Is Not an Endurance Test

There are a lot of rewards from knowing yourself. You are released from the pressure of unreasonable expectations. You no longer have to be weird inside because you are like everyone else outside. Sex is removed from the realm of partly being an ordeal or an endurance test. It becomes more of a magnificent challenge through which you can learn to express and enjoy all your desires.

Honestly!

One key to sexually expanding most relationships is the willingness to relate in the present, in what is actually happening. This is easily disrupted by hopes for the future or subtle expectations for the other person. Honesty is one of the roads to the kingdom of intimacy, whether it is in a thirty year marriage or a one night stand. If both lovers openly share their enjoyment of each other, and don't make an issue out of what it means, they should have a satisfying and meaningful time together that feels good. With honesty, every sexual experience becomes real and valid.

The questions of romance and commitment are frequently answered by the depth of intimacy a couple reaches. Emotional sensitivity and physical loving are usually the words by which two people tell each other about their love. If they only talk about it they cannot say as much. Direct involvement will often succeed where words fail.

Accepting Special Preferences

When you or your lover admits a new desire it may seem disconnected from your usual sexuality if neither of you has ever done it before. This is an illusion. If you feel a need for something, it is part of you—even if it is a wish for

black stockings, a vibrator, anal intercourse, a spanking, etc. The existence of the desire shows that it has emotional content and is goal directed. If you and your partner admit your deeper desires with sensitivity, you can both enjoy the fun of trying something new. Take it lightly, whatever it is. Enjoy the warmth you share during the experience—and enjoy the new ways to climax that you discover.

Some people take sex very seriously. This is a common obstacle to trying new things. Too much seriousness implies that these people have fixed their image of what sex should and should not be. On the contrary, you might try telling each other some of your wildest fantasies. While you won't try every fantasy, it will give you more flexibility and confidence because you will know each other much better. Your relationship may well thrive on your new found provocativeness.

The more secrets you admit, the sooner you will reach fireworks and orgasmic explosions. Trust your instincts—don't hide them. When you explore your sexuality, sex will once again become new and involving. You will develop a wider perspective on what is natural and what is not. Some of your sexual hang-ups may disappear like the morning mist.

What if you want to say no to something? Of course you should say it. Few people want to do everything their imagination dreams up. You will be better off drawing a line where you want to stop. In all probability, however, your present line is too tight. It may be choking off either pleasure or genuine self-expression.

Overcoming Embarrassment

You may feel embarrassed over something new that you really want to try. Overcoming embarrassment is much easier when you are with a person who loves you. It is mostly a matter of growing up and getting rid of your insecurity. Try to be more courageous, even if it means you have to shout at yourself inside or ask your lover for reassurance. So what? A bit of embarrassment is easier if it is shared. It is certainly worth the freedom to be yourself and feel pleasure.

Uninhibited Sex Games

What are some new things you might try?

The Joy of Narcissus: Large mirrors are great. They get better all the time since you become more willing to look openly. Once you become uninhibited, you might try holding a small mirror between your legs so you can both watch up close.

The Blindfold Game: One person is blind-folded and one is not. The kind of game you play determines who wears the blindfold and why. If you like to laugh, the blindfolded person can be the active partner and you can attempt something outrageous. Those who prefer dominance-submission can make the blindfolded person passive. Flip a coin in either case. You both have fantasies and *somebody* has to decide what you will do.

The Fetish Game: Set two dates a month from now and a week apart from each other. Each partner is responsible for one evening, and all their plans must be kept secret. Each fantasizes a fetish of their own, plans an evening around it, and purchases everything that will be needed. Write out the fantasy for the evening in detail, and include it in the gift-wrapped box that contains what you have bought. Start the evening by giving your lover this delicious gift. This is a great way to introduce a wide variety of clothing, paddles, dildoes, satiny materials, ropes, and other fun gimmicks that will probably turn out to be surprisingly pleasurable—simply because you want them. In a few months, "What's your latest fetish?" may be answered by a sinister but happy chuckle, a knowing wink, and the answer, "Saturday's going to be an unbelievable evening, honey."

Hot Bubbles: Bring a bottle of champagne or wine into a hot bubble bath with you and your lover. Finish the bottle in less than 45 minutes. During that time dream up the most appealing sexual fantasy the two of you can imagine. Then get out of the tub, dry yourselves, and do it! The chance to relax and talk, alone together, with wine, love, and laughter, makes the game's beginning both intimate and enjoyable. If you have outrageous imaginations, be prepared to laugh your way through the rest of it!

Discovery: This is a challenging way to enjoy the outdoors. Kiss, touch, or make love in a variety of places. Impulsively invent new ones. For example, the urge might strike in the car. Try going behind a low hedge just off the road. There are also bushes in parks, exit stairs in office buildings, and the offices themselves. There are beaches, tiny parks behind museums, and out-of-the-way alcoves at weddings. You don't have to go all the way—kissing and touching for a few minutes is fun. The challenge is its spontaneity and concealment. When will the impulse strike next? That's the question—until it happens!

The Big Tease: In this game one partner sexually stimulates the other into near agony, then brings them to total release. The partner being teased is undressed seductively and then tied face up on a bed. The active partner undresses himself or herself while kneeling and rubbing against the one who is tied—or standing over them, making them watch. Begin by touching them all over. Alternate light and firm pressures to sensitize their skin. Then focus on their erogenous zones and genitals. Kiss them from their mouth to their genitals. Also kneel so that they can kiss and lick yours. The trick—which may take several tries to perfect—is to excite your partner to a high plateau, then back off, then take them to a higher plateau. Keep stepping their excitement up, but always stop before they come. When the person who is tied just about can't stand it any more, bring them off. Then untie them immediately so that their muscles don't cramp. The one who was tied will probably want to make love again—all that teasing will usually drive their sexual appetite to a high pitch.

Against the Prejudice Against Middle-Aged Women

Neither men nor women lose their sexual desire as they age. Middle-aged men frequently date women half their age. Why can't women do the same? In fact, it is doubtful that liberated young women in their 20's will accept today's lack of sexual freedom when they reach their 40's and 50's. Why shouldn't this discrimination disappear now?

Many women, like many men, become better lovers as they reach middle age. A touch of gray, a little fat, a couple of stretch marks, and a few wrinkles are not valid reasons for sexual discrimination. They are signs of experience as much as age. Most middle-aged men obviously aren't ideal examples of youthful beauty. Human beings are like wine: some age poorly, most very well. Those who have matured and learned warmth, kindness, and understanding should have every opportunity to love fully and be loved in return—no matter what their sex or age. Anything less is a loss to our whole society.

Sharing Desires

The importance of good sexual communication cannot be stressed enough, because it can produce all that lovers search for. Don't be afraid to whisper, "I want it slow and sensuous tonight," or, "Let's try a fantasy that's been driving me wild all week." Being able to tell your lover all you want is the way you become your real sexual self. If you fake it and stay hidden inside, you are cheating your relationship, your lover, and yourself.

Don't expect fireworks or an explosive orgasm when you try something new. The first time is often better when it is sensitive and understanding, whether it is a new technique or a new lover. You can let go completely once you learn the territory. Sharing a new experience with your lover is fun, and the intimacy you develop expands the ecstasy you will soon enjoy.

Enjoying Both "Hot" and "Cool" Sex

There are two kinds of "hot" sex. The first is to be avoided. This is when you are anxious and rush through intercourse, hoping for a successful conclusion. The second kind of hot sex is desirable. It is when you let go completely and release all the passion inside.

"Cool" sex is gentle and permitted. It is slow, easy and natural. The pleasure is deepened gradually. Each partner shares the lead in loving the other. Deep emotions and sensitivity predominate. Performance is secondary—until the end, when wildness takes over.

"Good" hot sex is fun. Heat things up (if you are a woman) by becoming a smoldering beauty with a neckline plunged to the navel. Or (if you are a man), dress up as a seductive Valentino and ply her with enough whiskey and no-holds barred kisses to make her throw her last inhibition to the winds.

Good cool sex can reawaken and intensify your love. Plan ahead and set aside an evening, a day, or a weekend. Buy enough wine and take a vacation in bed with each other. Search together for the emotional depths that making it slow can produce.

Need a New Hobby?

As your sexuality develops you will discover truly beautiful moments. You can preserve vivid memories of your unrestrained passion, humor, originality, and affection with a Polaroid camera. The best adventures you've enjoyed can be saved in a private photo album. Sudden impulses may strike when you look at your pictures together. You may jump into each other's arms and bring your best memories back to life.

Several precautions are important. Don't use a regular camera and send the film to a lab for developing. Second, keep your intimate pictures private. It's embarrassing when the wrong picture pops up at the wrong time. The last rule is best. Wait an hour after undressing before taking pictures. The marks clothes make on the skin fade slowly. If you use this time to make love, the afterglow gives your pictures a special quality that makes them twice as memorable.

The Challenges of Success

Being genuine plays a large part in sexual success. Pretenses do not last long: when you love, you inevitably bring your whole self to bed. If you are trying to hide something, this eventually becomes obvious. The person who loves you knows you for who you are, even if you think they don't. And they love you anyway.

Emotional or physical problems are not excuses to fail. Everyone has problems of one kind or another. The pleasure you create is more important than the kind of problems you have.

When you do succeed, success doesn't turn out to be a magic pill. You feel good when it happens but life remains the same. There are two main options: the precious and the precarious,

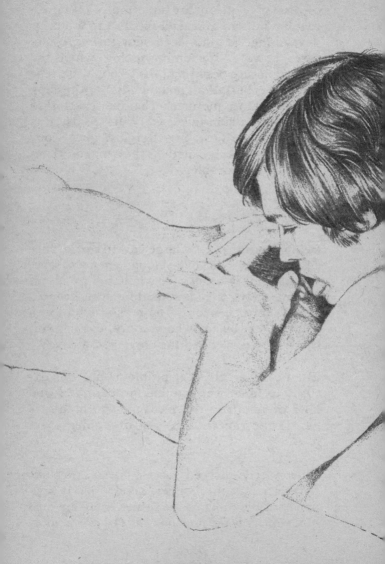

and you have to cope with both of them. The first is to hold on to the love you have found, to rejoice in the transcendence you share, to give and receive, to support and to be made to feel secure.

The second option is more complex. An individual life can be seen as eternally precarious. You started with a dream of love, reached it, and enjoyed it. Life goes on. You certainly have more dreams. You must choose between the dream you have or risk it in the attempt to reach the other dreams you want but do not possess. How much is enough? How tight is your gut twisted by the dreams you have not yet reached?

There is a challenge hidden in the most satisfying successes, an inevitable part of the mystery of being human: when do you say, "Enough! This is the dream I want for the rest of my life!"?

The Great Semen-Swallowing Debate

Is the taste of semen addicting? It depends on you. Some women find it irresistible. Others can take it or leave it. Some don't like it. Where do you stand? The best way to find out is by a sensual experiment. After all, he tastes her juices—or perhaps drowns himself in them —all the time. The first time he tasted a woman it was very sensual.

He should begin by going down on her. Kneel next to her shoulders. While he kisses her she should play with him. When they are both turned on, he can lie on his side facing her. Kiss each other, going easy at first. Concentrate on each other's best "spots." Build the intensity as high as it will go. He should give her one or more orgasms before he reaches his climax. Arrange a signal beforehand so he can tell her just before he comes. This can be a simple tap on the shoulder, or he can pull her hips fiercely against his face and bury his tongue inside her. Then plunge ahead to the finish. It may help her if she wraps three or more fingers tight around the base of his penis so she can feel the spurts as they come. If she pulls away, she should hold his penis tight until his orgasm is finished. Whatever happens, make love at least once more that night—the usual way. This kind of an evening, if done with the right attitude, can be intimate and enjoyable—no matter how it turns out.

Another first time way is for her to nurse him gently for 45 minutes to an hour, while he lightly touches her all over. Climaxing is not the point of this hour. Building a total rapport and closeness is.

Gentle Loving

The gentleness in lovemaking is more than the way you touch. It is the quality of your feeling

for each other. The point of a large fraction of sex is to develop a complete acceptance of each other and yourself. An important part of this is not to expect "superior performance." Having a good time and sharing a bond of intimacy will increase the vitality of your sexual relationship more than a "big" orgasm. The experiences that bring two lovers close emotionally count for more in the long run than the techniques that get them off the quickest.

Developing this kind of complete acceptance can lead full circle, back to the "bigger" orgasm. With this much intimacy lovers can openly teach and guide each other in the midst of lovemaking. They can take each other's hand, mouth, hips, etc. and put it just where they want it, gently guiding their partner in the motions that are most exciting. There isn't time for lengthy explanations in the middle of intercourse. Direct physical guidance can improve the quality of sex considerably, since each partner is constantly teaching the other the specific stimulations that excite them the most.

New, Wilder Standards

Yesterday's and today's sexual values will continue to change rapidly. There recently emerged a widespread and disenchantment with the dependent and passive wife role. Homosexuality has come out of the closet, bisexuality and swinging are spreading, babies are wanted out of wedlock, men and women live together without marrying, divorce has become an epidemic, and the search for full sexual satisfaction rushes forward in the "conventional" marriages that remain.

These sexual freedoms are part of a new standard that is just as strong as the old standard in many ways. The difference is that the new one is wider ranging. More people live outside the norm of the lifetime nuclear family, and they have demanded their full rights as legitimate human beings. Today, when a woman finds the right person for a lover—gentle, considerate, and understanding—they might enjoy breast sucking, oral foreplay and total satiation . . . without a man entering the bedroom.

The question is not whether these changes are good or bad. They will accelerate no matter what judgment anyone sets on them. The real question is whether people can control themselves enough to receive the benefits of freedom without paying an excessive price.

How Do You Love More Than One?

There are many kinds of love. There's cool love and hot love, love for friends, passionate one nighters, the sudden ecstasy of loving a woman or man half your age, and the intimacy of twenty years of marriage. The proof that a man and a woman can love more than each other comes (quietly, in secret) each day (in affairs). It is proved by swinging couples, by marriages

that accept a third lover, by happy promiscuous singles, and by millions who marry someone new every few years. Is all this crazy? Maybe not. Maybe for today's human beings, this is normal.

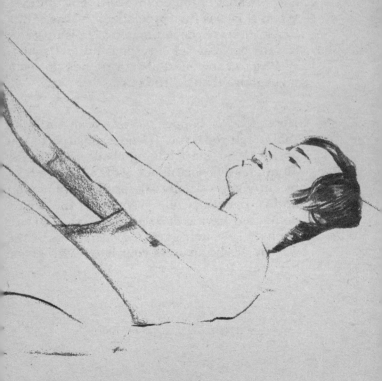

In the midst of all this loving, each individual should be picky. Otherwise falling in love again and again becomes ordinary and not the supremely special thing that it can be. How do you love more than one? Easily—but selectively.

Are Friends Lovers?

Some people enjoy sex with a variety of partners without falling in love with any of them. When this was first proclaimed it was called free love. It is a consummated friendship without any permanence or responsibility. Usually, getting to know most of your friends this well takes more than a little guts.

How does it happen? First, your intuition should tell you if your friend is sensitive to you or not. If so, start talking about sexy topics. Mention any books about sex that you've read recently and casually ask for their opinion on nudity, frequency of orgasm, what they enjoy doing and having done to them, etc. You can often judge your friend's responsiveness by the way he or she answers your looks with his or her eyes.

Reviving a Marriage

There are two routes to reviving a marriage sexually: in or out of the marriage. Either can be essential to preserving the relationship, since many couples' sex lives seem to slip in quality very quickly.

The suggestions in the second and third chapters of this book may give some couples new ways to expand their lovemaking. Whatever they try, the key is to enjoy their intimacy enough that sex together begins to feel very good again.

The other alternative is to add spice by going outside the marriage. The trick is to reawaken desires that will recharge the primary relationship. Bring your stronger sexuality home, and you may find the love affair you have been looking for.

Many marriages are broken up by a husband or wife who is sexually dissatisfied. However you reawaken your sex life, it is better than not acting at all and letting the marriage fail.

Is It True Swingers Have More Fun?

Swinging is not a suburban social club. It is a spectrum in which you can pick what satisfies you best. You may prefer the intimacy of two couples watching each other make love. The ways to love are as varied as people. You can

ask questions, think about the answers, and learn from new attitudes. Two couples do not have to swap partners. Their goal can be intimacy and sensuality, not peak excitement.

The next step is changing partners. There are many reasons cited: emancipation, sexual restlessness, rejection of the double standard for men, a realization that serial monogamy with adultery is the same thing hidden, or a desire to enjoy new partners without sacrificing the primary relationship. As a result, swinging can be based on honesty and mutual concern as well as simple, straightforward lust. It can be "open" with everyone in the same room, or "closed" where couples swap partners and have sex in separate rooms.

If it is in the same room it can be hot or cool. When it is cool couples make love tenderly, usually fairly conventionally, with attention to each other's sensitivities. When it is hot it is quite another scene.

Imagine that you are in a dimly lit room. Within reach is more of everything you've ever wanted to touch than you can handle. You feel humping bodies on all sides, slide your fingers along them, following the pulses to their source. Meanwhile you are either making love with your mouth and hips, or being loved passionately.

In general, swinging does not involve many couples furiously making it together. It is usually two or three couples who either swap and go into separate bedrooms or make love gently while they are together. Picking the wrong kind of couple can be a bad experience. Fortunately, people are usually the same with their clothes on or off. Anyone who doesn't have some sensitivity and warmth, who doesn't increase your couple-closeness, or who won't relate to you as a whole person is a bad choice for intimacy.

Watch Out for the Overcrowded Bed

There is a "no!" side to swinging. Some people are casual swingers and others are not. If you aren't casual about sex, don't go to any "parties" since they will be disastrous experiences for you—though everyone else might enjoy themselves.

The $90-a-Year Love Affair

Many marriages have an "adequate" sex life, but it isn't anything special. The man often thinks that if he has an erection that's all his wife needs to be satisfied. To him, a terrific evening is if he has three orgasms—he feels just like a teenager again. What about her? He may be a good provider, help around the house and be great with the kids, but he treats her like a wife, not a lover. She probably hasn't had an orgasm in years.

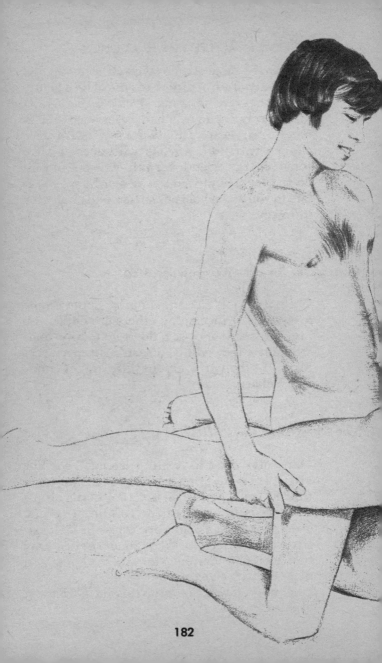

Would you believe that ninety dollars a year might turn that marriage into a torrid, zinging love affair? Here's how: if he would go out of his way once a month to buy his wife a little gift as a surprise and give it to her with feeling and affection, making love to her that night the way she wants to be loved, she would be in heaven. It can be as little as a humorous card, a small potted plant, a sculpted candle, a bottle of wine, an occasional bouquet of flowers, or a rare romantic dinner out. Ninety dollars a year averages out to $7.50 a month, which is enough to surprise her fairly often.

To a woman in love, indifference is a man's greatest sin. It can kill her love faster than anything else, even faster than pain and anguish. Don't promise her anything. Show her. She'll know she's loved when you start bringing her small gifts and making love romantically. It won't be long before this marriage turns back into a love affair.

Heavy Extra-Marital Relationships

One of the supposed benefits of marriage is that it gives two people the opportunity to share any sexual experience that is mutually pleasurable. This doesn't always work. One partner may be preoccupied by a desire or a fantasy and their partner won't even try it. There may be other problems, such as her failure to reach a climax. He may take this personally and seek extra-marital relationships to prove that it is her fault and not his own. She, in turn, may find other men because he has become unfeeling.

A heavy extra-marital relationship is usually evidence that something is wrong with the primary relationship. Whatever the problem is, it should be faced and dealt with before it grows larger. These husbands and wives are long overdue for frank and honest communication. If they actually tried to find out what is wrong and patiently tried to solve it together, making clear how serious a problem it is, this might drastically alter their relationship for the better.

We Are the Future and in Spite of Problems We Work

Sexual desire appears to be expanding almost more rapidly than society can cope with it. In the past most couples didn't know they had to turn each other on. They just banged away until he was done. Now we know how limited this was. Tenderness, affection, and a great deal of patient touching, kissing, and sensuality will make practically anyone sexually aggressive.

Staying Together in the Middle of Changes

Obviously, our society is continuing to loosen up morally. This is a difficult time for those who cannot handle freedom. Every person has to learn where to draw the line for himself. What is great for one person may be bad for someone else. Sex is certainly fulfilling and important, but it has to be measured and tailored to each individual's preferences. With honesty, the ability to learn from experience, open communications, and the willingness to draw the line at whatever boundary you set for yourself, you can let go and enjoy a wide variety of sexual experiences within your limits.

Quantity Does Not Replace Quality

Increased and more honest sexuality can be a boon to society, but it is the speed with which sexuality is opening up that causes the greatest worries. More is only sometimes better. The how and why are just as important as the quantity. The easiest way to tell if you have substituted quantity for quality is if no one with whom you go to bed satisfies you completely. Then the problem lies in the quantity, not in your lovemaking—which might be in-

credible if you opened up to one person. The satisfaction will most likely return in a serious love affair with the person you care about most.

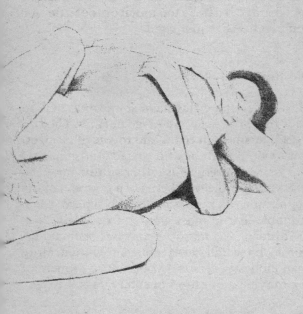

The X-Rated Motel

For a lust-filled night or a hedonistic weekend, the X-rated motel is spreading up and down America's coasts and moving inward from there. Naked lovers lie on fur-covered water beds and watch pornographic movies on closed circuit television. Three-speed vibrators are often available. Large mirrors usually hang on the walls and ceilings. Is this going too far? As usual, its what you do with it that counts. It can be too much or too little—or you can make it just right.

There's No Business Like . . .

Most American cities have something new to offer these days . . . massage parlors. They do a good business in cities and towns of all sizes. It is obvious that they fill a need, and commercial sex between consenting adults may be necessary for the well being of a segment of the population. As rape increases to where it is a palpable fear in most women from New York to California, some outlet may be necessary for those who would harm innocent women. More than honesty versus hypocrisy, commercial sex may be a question of safety versus rape.

This is a Promethean dilemma: the gift of sexual fire has become one of the strongest forces shaping the American way of life. It breaks up marriages and families, makes many dissatisfied with themselves, and promises, a happier, more fulfilled society.

Bon Voyeurage!

Sex is an elemental human force that has assumed many faces across the centuries and in different societies. Primitive or refined, we are all submerged in a torrent of sexual urges.

We have entered an age of sexual experimentation that compares to few others in history. The torrent itself has overflowed the cultural levees that contained its force. It is searching for new, more natural channels in which to flow.

An individual life is insubstantial. After death, it is as if any one person had never been born. It is the sexual torrent that endures—yet this transcendent force lives through individuals. It brings every person into life through their parents. This should be all it need give, but the torrent compels everyone to give and accept love, and this produces the essence of humanity. The attempt to find love generates restlessness, arousal, persistance, acceptance of personal limitations, and growth to maturity. The discovery of love brings sensitivity, empathy, sincerity, affection, and the admission of responsibility.

The sexual torrent is the force behind individual existence, and the force that compels people to reach their emotional pinnacle. Without it, our hearts and souls would be empty, if they could exist at all. Dance in the torrent for it dances in you.